HANNah
SYLAO

TIGER SWALLOWTAIL BUTTERFLY ALIGHTS IN MAINE'S BAXTER STATE PARK.
FOLLOWING PAGES: CLOUDS HOVER OVER PROPOSED GREAT BURN WILDERNESS ON IDAHO-MONTANA BORDER.

America's Hidden Wilderness
Lands of Seclusion

Prepared by the Special Publications Division
National Geographic Society, Washington, D.C.

AMERICA'S HIDDEN WILDERNESS
Lands of Seclusion

Contributing Authors: THOMAS B. ALLEN,
  GEORGE F. MOBLEY, JAMES RAFFAN,
  CYNTHIA RUSS RAMSAY, SCOTT THYBONY,
  SUZANNE VENINO, S. JEFFREY K. WILKERSON
Contributing Photographers: CRAIG AURNESS,
  TOM BEAN, JONATHAN S. BLAIR,
  RICHARD ALEXANDER COOKE III, DAVID HISER,
  GEORGE F. MOBLEY, PHILIP SCHERMEISTER,
  MICHAEL S. YAMASHITA

Published by THE NATIONAL GEOGRAPHIC SOCIETY
GILBERT M. GROSVENOR,
  President and Chairman of the Board
MELVIN M. PAYNE, THOMAS W. MCKNEW,
  Chairmen Emeritus
OWEN R. ANDERSON, Executive Vice President
ROBERT L. BREEDEN, Senior Vice President,
  Publications and Educational Media

Prepared by THE SPECIAL PUBLICATIONS DIVISION
DONALD J. CRUMP, Director
PHILIP B. SILCOTT, Associate Director
BONNIE S. LAWRENCE, Assistant Director

Staff for this book
THOMAS B. ALLEN, Managing Editor
CHARLES E. HERRON, Illustrations Editor
JODY BOLT, Art Director
BARBARA PAYNE, Project Planner
  and Senior Researcher
SALLIE M. GREENWOOD, Researcher
RICHARD M. CRUM, ROSAMUND GARNER,
  JANE MCCAULEY, THOMAS O'NEILL,
  JAMES RAFFAN, CYNTHIA RUSS RAMSAY,
  SCOTT THYBONY, SUZANNE VENINO,
  Picture Legend Writers
JOHN D. GARST, JR., VIRGINIA L. BAZA,
  JUDITH F. BELL, SVEN M. DOLLING,
  GARY M. JOHNSON, DANIEL J. ORTIZ,
  TIBOR G. TOTH, MARTIN S. WALZ,
  Map Research and Production
RICHARD M. CRUM, H. ROBERT MORRISON,
  Editorial Consultants
ROSAMUND GARNER, Editorial Assistant
ARTEMIS S. LAMPATHAKIS, Illustrations Assistant

Engraving, Printing, and Production Manufacture
GEORGE V. WHITE, Manager,
  Manufacturing and Quality Management
VINCENT P. RYAN, Assistant Manager,
  Manufacturing and Quality Management
DAVID V. SHOWERS, Production Manager
LEWIS R. BASSFORD, Assistant Production Manager
KATHY CIRUCCI, TIMOTHY H. EWING,
  Senior Production Assistants
KEVIN P. HEUBUSCH, Production Assistant
CAROL R. CURTIS, Senior Production Staff Assistant
SUSAN A. BENDER, BETSY ELLISON,
  MARISA FARABELLI, KAYLENE KAHLER,
  KAREN KATZ, ELIZA MORTON,
  SANDRA F. LOTTERMAN, DRU STANCAMPIANO,
  Staff Assistants
MAUREEN WALSH, Indexer

PHILIP SCHERMEISTER (BELOW) HARDCOVER AND DUST JACKET: JESS R. LEE

ESSENCE OF A HIDDEN WILDERNESS: A BROOK RUMBLES THROUGH AN

EVER-CHANGING PATTERN OF LIGHT AND SHADOW IN BAXTER STATE PARK, MAINE.

UNDAUNTED BY DRIVING RAIN AND TURBULENT WATER, MARK SCRIVER AND BOWMAN RIK COOKE

PADDLE TO ADVENTURE IN NORTHERN QUEBEC.

7

Foreword

In West Virginia, where I come from, we have given wilderness a second chance. Forests logged over long ago have come back as wild lands newborn in the National Wilderness Preservation System. One such place is the Dolly Sods Wilderness, a gem on Allegheny Mountain in northeastern West Virginia. You can find blueberries there, and, in the bogs, cranberries and orchids. Spruces, shaped by wind and cold, look like green flags stiff before an eternally steady breeze.

Dolly Sods, named for a family that once worked its sods, or meadows, is not large by the system's standards. The protected plateau covers little more than 10,000 acres; many other wildernesses in the system have acreage measured in the millions. But Dolly Sods looms large in the memories of the people who have discovered it. And that is one of the gifts of wilderness: No matter its size or fame, it remains hidden until you enter and discover it for yourself.

Wilderness awes us. Roaming through a realm beyond the everyday, we know we find far more there than the beauty of lake or mountain, far more than the birdsong or the whispers of a desert night. People of every era and every culture have known that feeling of beyond, and all have tried to express it. "My words are tied in one with the great mountains, with the great rocks, with the great trees," said the Yokuts, a tribe that lived in what would be California. Long after the Yokuts, John Muir tied his words to what he experienced in that land. "The clearest way into the Universe," he wrote, "is through a forest wilderness."

Each of us has a different sense of wilderness. To a backpacker, wilderness is solitude, earned by a daylong hike. To a canoeist on a rampaging river, wilderness is adventure. To an ecologist plunging into a tropical rain forest, wilderness is scientific discovery. And to a reader, wilderness is a place known through the senses of others, through images tied to the mountains and the rocks and the trees.

Our sampler of wilderness spans North America from the Arctic to the tropics. A pair of backpackers find—and lose—a trail in Maine's North Woods. Tropical researchers penetrate Mexico's imperiled Lacandon Forest. In a hidden Utah canyon, hikers trek through a forgotten past. Surefooted horses carry high-country campers into the Great Burn, a fire-ravaged swath of the Bitterroots that, like Dolly Sods, came back. A veteran Far North traveler discovers the magic of an Arctic spring. The Mojave, which motorists usually speed through and ignore, unveils its beauty to a desert wanderer. Backbreaking portages and clouds of mosquitoes confront voyagers on Canada's Rivière à l'Eau Claire.

North America's cities have not paved over all the wild places. Canada supports more than 800 national and provincial parks, which protect more than 93 million acres of wild lands. The U.S. Wilderness Act of 1964 put about 9 million acres into a realm "where the earth and its community of life are untrammeled by man, where man himself is a visitor who does not remain." Now, not quite a quarter-century later, more than 89 million

From North America's diverse lands comes a wilderness panorama: tundra, river, woodland, desert, mountain, canyon, and tropical rain forest.

acres are protected. Other U.S. wildernesses are preserved in private holdings and in public parks, forests, and wildlife refuges.

Mexico's wildernesses cannot be readily measured, for many of her wild lands are retreating before constantly shifting frontiers. Mexico, with a population density nearly twice that of the United States and 15 times that of Canada, does not view wilderness the way its northern neighbors do. Mexico looks upon its jungles as wild lands to be tamed. On the scales of economics, development usually must outweigh preservation. But, as jungles shrivel and rivers are dammed, some Mexicans have begun asking where and when the bulldozers will stop.

Don Miguel Alvarez del Toro, an outstanding Mexican naturalist, in 1985 received a medal from the Mexican Institute of Natural Resources. He politely thanked the government agency for the award—but pointedly added that he would have preferred the purchase and protection of even a square meter of endangered land. His feeling for wilderness echoes the prayer of the Maya who once lived in his beloved Lacandon Forest. They believed that the gods created the people of the dawn to be what we all should be today—"a supporter, a nourisher" of earth.

ROBERT L. BREEDEN
Senior Vice President, Publications and Educational Media

By Thomas B. Allen

Photographs by Philip Schermeister

Quest for Solitude

Spotting Berries and Moose in Maine's North Woods

Still waters, evergreen forests, and a mountain skyline enframe the tranquil wilderness of Maine's Baxter State Park, run as a realm "where nature rules."

When we finally admitted we were lost, we stopped, took off our packs, sat on a log, and backtracked in memory. The trail along the lake had led us to the logging road. Two hours later the road had vanished, leaving us at the edge of a dense thicket. Through the tangle of brush and fallen trees we had seen a blue ribbon tied around a spruce. Deeper in the gloom, other blue ribbons had beckoned. So we had plunged into the woods, bushwhacking from one ribbon to the next.

For the past three days my wife, Scottie, and I had followed trusty blue-paint blazes to idyllic campsites. The blue ribbons, we thought, would soon lead us back to the blue blazes of the permanent trail. Now, sitting on our log, we realized we had walked in the wrong direction for at least two and a half hours.

We were in the middle of the last day of a four-day hike along the northernmost trail in Baxter State Park, a Maine wilderness that had seemed ideal for our first backpacking trip. We had hiked and camped many times before. Never, though, had we packed our camp on our backs and carried it from place to place. Baxter, its forests fringed by picnic grounds and tranquil ponds, did not appear a forbidding wilderness for a pair of tyros. So, well in advance, we had made reservations for campsites.

On a typical summer's day, Baxter's gatekeepers let fewer than a thousand people into the park's 314 square miles of forest and mountain. Most people hike, picnic, or stop at drive-in campgrounds. All campers must have reservations. In the backcountry, the strict controls protect trails from eroding overuse. They also guarantee that at the end of the day backpackers will not find interlopers in the trailside lean-tos or tentsites. Rangers hand prospective campers a list of regulations that help keep Baxter the way its charter intended. It is supposed to be a "sanctuary for wild beasts and birds," not a conventional park catering to human needs.

Baxter mixes the typical fare of a state park—picnic grounds and easy day hikes—with the tough mountain ascents and trackless forest of a true wilderness. It is also a place of visible moose and elusive trout, of waterfalls and serene ponds. Most of all, it is a place of few people.

Baxter gave us solitude, along with moments that told us we were not alone. One day a young moose ambled toward us on the trail. All three of us froze, startled by the encounter. We saw moose at other times. But the warblers flitting about, trilling their quick songs, were usually invisible. So were the woodpeckers, rat-tat-tatting on the dead white trees thrusting through the green surrounding us.

For three days the trail had taken us where we had wanted to go—far from our ordinary world. Lost and without a trail, we began to lose our enthusiasm for seclusion. Baxter's solitude had become isolation. We were on our own.

Our compass showed that the blue ribbons we had been following had led us northeast when we should have been heading southeast. Our map did not show the logging road, although we had been told to expect one. Our reading of the map put us in the middle of Wadleigh Bog. We had been struggling, far off course, toward what the mapmaker had prophetically named Blunder Pond.

Until now we had had little need for the map of Baxter State Park. The Freezeout Trail had been easy to follow from our start at Trout Brook Farm Campground northward to Webster Stream. Then it veered westward, alongside that wild, cascading water, to the glimmering peace and mournful loons of Webster Lake.

At Trout Brook on the first night, in the wan shadows cast by a moon nearing full, we had stood by our tent and heard the soft voices of two unseen fishermen hauling up their canoe for the night. Long, thin clouds were skittering across the moon when we crawled into our sleeping bags. So lovely was the shrouded night we forgot the price of clouds is often rain.

Next day, trying to ignore the downpours, we had breakfast, broke camp, packed, and set out. Rain dogged us for most of the ten miles to our next stop, a lean-to on the bank of Webster Stream. From the campground to the stream we walked an old lumber road, a reminder that the forests here had known loggers long before hikers. Parts of several Baxter trails follow traces of tote roads, once used for hauling in supplies, and logging roads, built for the sleds that hauled out logs. At one spot, just off the trail, we had tramped a huge hill of sawdust, a relic of a vanished mill.

Baxter's trails offer a great variety of experience to the sole: mud, moss, peat, flinty rock, the stepping-stones across a brook, a zigzag split-log track built across a bog, a logging road's corduroy of buried, moldering logs. You watch your step on a forest trail, and this induces tunnel vision, an ever-changing view of the near at hand. You are rewarded not by vistas but by small surprises.

A web spans a sunny patch of trail, and suddenly you are eye-to-eye with a spider. Looking down, you may see the heart-shaped hoofprint of a moose, the scat of a bear. Looking to left or right, you see a fern nibbled by a deer or a moss-draped rock crowned by a tiny forest. And there are the berries, those luscious berries. Scottie was particularly good at spotting raspberries and lowbush blueberries along the trail. Sometimes we had to kneel to reach the blueberries, which grow so low that spruce grouse can waddle along, berry-picking without craning their necks.

Pick-sit-and-eat berry harvesting continually interrupted our strict hiking schedule. We had planned five minutes of rest for every thirty minutes of walking. But we had not anticipated the berries—or the blowdowns. For long stretches these storm-felled trees made the trail an obstacle course we navigated by climbing, crawling, or log-walking. I wondered what the Freezeout must have been like when it got its name. Lumbermen took the trail in winter when icy lakes were unsafe for travel. Then as now, Freezeout led to the tote road, which in lumbering days ended at the food and warmth of Trout Brook Farm, a provisioner for lumber camps.

Freezeout arcs across the top of Baxter, far from the park's centerpiece, the colossal splendor of Mount Katahdin. The trail encompasses within its 15 miles a vast green sampler of the Maine North Woods. Here campsites are few and people rare. Far more moose, deer, and bear use the trail than two-legged hikers. We were two days on the trail before we saw another human being. In four days we saw four people.

Our first day on the trail ended at a lean-to looking down on a broad, slow-flowing run of Webster Stream. The rain had stopped. I snapped some dead lower branches off a spruce. With this dry kindling and some wood picked from the ground and stripped of its soggy bark, I built a fire big enough for cooking and the drying of soaked shirts, boots, and socks.

Next morning, we got wet again, this time voluntarily. The water was cold, the sun bright and warm. Tiny fish explored our toes. There in the stream we lived some of those inconsequential moments that become life-long memories.

Our journey that day was short, about five miles along Webster Stream to its source, Webster Lake. There we found a tentsite tucked into a stand of young spruce about ten yards from the stony lakeshore. We spent a sunny afternoon swimming, gathering driftwood, and picking raspberries and blackberries.

We cooked our dinner at a permanent fixture of the campsite, a circular fireplace made of large stones. The grill consisted of a rusty wagon wheel hub and three iron spikes, each a foot and a half long. The spikes once had held together a timber dam somewhere nearby. Lumbermen built the dams to control the waterways on which logs began their voyage from forest to mill. The wagon wheels probably had rolled along a tote road serving the lumber camps.

The Freezeout Trail ended near our tentsite. We followed the trail the next morning along the lakeshore and then picked up the Webster Lake Trail. It curved southward for about seven miles to the gravel road that loops around the park and provides access to many of the hiking trails. We were then to hike the road about seven miles to a final campsite, near where we had started three days before. But that is not how we did it.

The northwest corner of the park includes a large swath of forest called the Scientific Forest Management Area. The Webster Lake Trail, we had been told, partially follows an old logging road through the area. We had followed another road, hacked out of the forest more recently and not completed. We had veered into that northward curving road and had followed the blue ribbons staking its future course.

We did not know this during our conference on the log. All we knew was that we had to figure how to get ourselves from this unknown place to a known one. That was the doctrine of Henry David Thoreau, who in 1857 had searched for a companion near Webster Lake—a landscape "made out of Chaos and Old Night." When the missing man appeared after a hungry night in the woods, Thoreau calmly welcomed him as more late than lost. (An editor, footnoting this incident, remarked that a true woodsman is never lost, even though he "on occasion may not know just where he is.")

Although we certainly did not know where we were, our map showed us a way to known places. A southward course would most likely take us to

Homeland of moose, deer, bear, fox, and numerous bird species, Baxter State Park encompasses 201,018 acres of North Woods wilderness. The park's tallest mountain, 5,267-foot Katahdin, anchors the northern end of the Appalachian Trail. Some 160 miles of other trails attract hikers and backpackers.

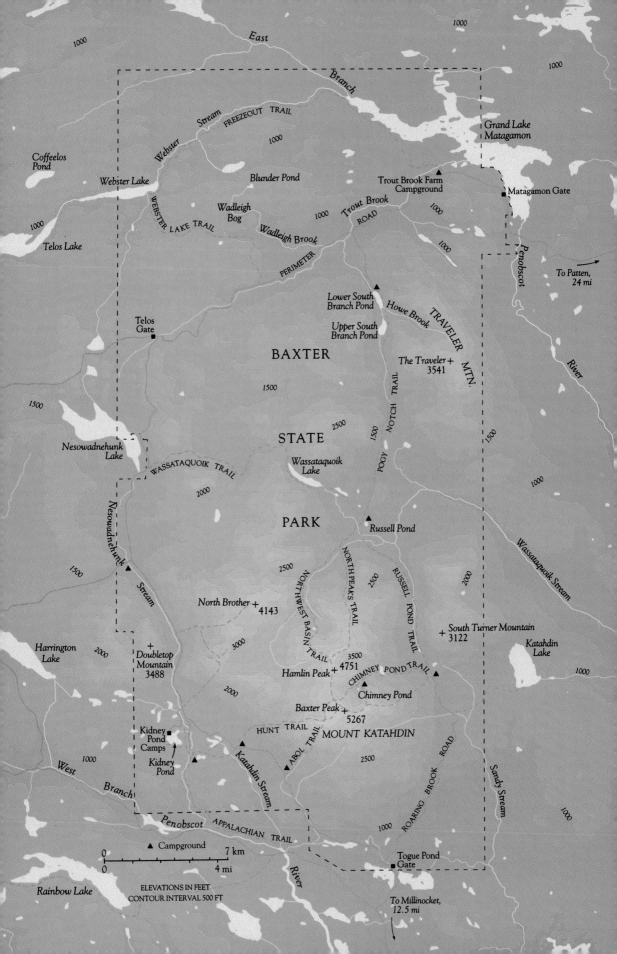

1000

East

1000

Branch

1000

FREEZEOUT TRAIL

Stream

Webster

1000

Grand Lake
Matagamon

Coffeelos
Pond

Webster Lake

Blunder Pond

Trout Brook Farm
Campground

1000

Matagamon Gate

WEBSTER LAKE TRAIL

Wadleigh
Bog

Trout Brook

1000

Telos Lake

1000

Wadleigh Brook

ROAD

1000

To Patten,
24 mi

PERIMETER

1000

Penobscot

Lower South
Branch Pond

Howe Brook

TRAVELER MTN.

Telos
Gate

Upper South
Branch Pond

River

BAXTER

The Traveler +
3541

1500

POGY NOTCH TRAIL

1500

Nesowadnehunk
Lake

STATE

2500

1500

WASSATAQUOIK TRAIL

Wassataquoik
Lake

2000

1000

PARK

Russell Pond

Wassataquoik Stream

1500

Nesowadnehunk

2500

2500

NORTH PEAKS TRAIL

2200

RUSSELL POND TRAIL

2000

Harrington
Lake

2000

North Brother +
4143

NORTHWEST BASIN TRAIL

South Turner Mountain
+ 3122

Katahdin
Lake

1500

Stream

3000

3500

CHIMNEY POND TRAIL

1000

+
Doubletop
Mountain
3488

2000

Hamlin Peak +
4751

Chimney Pond

Kidney
Pond
Camps

HUNT TRAIL

ABOL TRAIL

Baxter Peak +
5267

MOUNT KATAHDIN

ROARING BROOK ROAD

West

1000

Kidney
Pond

Katahdin Stream

2500

Branch

Penobscot

APPALACHIAN TRAIL

1000

Sandy Stream

▲ Campground

7 km

Togue Pond
Gate

1000

Rainbow Lake

0 _____ 4 mi

ELEVATIONS IN FEET
CONTOUR INTERVAL 500 FT

River

To Millinocket,
12.5 mi

the Webster Lake Trail, part of which ran on a northwest-southeast tack. If we somehow missed the trail, by hiking south we still would emerge from the woods somewhere on the park's gravel road, which bisected the forest.

All I needed to do was set a bearing south. The procedure was simple: Stand in front of a tree, holding a compass in front of me. The double-arrowed needle is painted red for north, white for south. I line up the needle so the white arrow points toward a landmark. We walk to that landmark. When I get to it, I repeat the procedure. And so on for the five or six miles to the trail or, missing that, the seven or eight miles to the road.

What seemed so reasonable when I looked at a map turned out to be maddeningly difficult in the reality of Chaos and Old Night. The undergrowth of the forest was so thick I often had to line up my bearing on trees only 15 or 20 feet apart. We sometimes found ourselves in graveyards of windblown trees. Some of them, still thick with spiky branches, formed impassable barricades. Others, old and moss-barked, looked easy to clamber over but were hollow traps for an unwary foot.

In the bog, I had trouble even finding a tree to stand in front of. I often had to crouch on a hummock and peer through dank, bristling terrain that lacked trees, let alone landmarks. So I took a bearing on a bush on another hummock. Then, unable to reach it on a straight line, we slogged to the left or right and headed for my compass sighting sideways, hoping when we got there I had found the right bush on the right hummock.

The map showed that our southern bearing would take us out of the bog. While we did look forward to more light and less damp, the bog had been a help, for its sluggish brooks twice gave us water. We filled our canteens, added a double dose of water-purification tablets, and stopped worrying about dehydration.

The bog slowly disappeared, the squishy black soil giving way to moss and solid earth strewn with rocks, bumps, roots, and rotting logs. We were stumbling through woods darkly thick with trees and brush. Branches and vines whipped us and shredded the scant daylight leaking through the forest canopy. But wherever disease or storm had felled a towering spruce or fir, sunlight streamed down on a carpet of new growth—ground pine, stands of young white birch, ankle-high seedlings, clusters of wildflowers, huge fans of fern.

We reluctantly begrudged the beauty around us, for we had to crash our way through it, our thoughts on our lost trail, not the wonders of the wild. Bushwhacking is hard, sweaty work. And progress is difficult to measure. We estimated we were traveling, at best, half a mile an hour. We stopped frequently, to rest and to decide whether to continue doing what we had agreed to do: head south until we found the trail or the road.

In late afternoon, well out of the bog and sitting on a rock laced in yellow lichens, we began to weaken. We talked about making camp and resuming our trek in the morning. But we knew we had at least four hours of daylight, and we decided to keep on walking south.

At half past seven, about five and a half hours after we first suspected we were lost, Scottie spotted a break in the trees some 50 yards away. We stepped across the forest threshold and stood on a trail. I checked the map against the compass. This had to be the Webster Lake Trail.

We did not know where we were on the trail, but we knew if we kept walking south the trail would get us out. We hiked another thirty minutes. Then, with little light or energy left, we declared a mild emergency and changed our night's reservation to a site just off the trail. An owl and a couple of bats treated us to a flyover just before we fell asleep.

In the morning we walked to the trailhead. Like most of the trails, this one ended at what the founder of Baxter called the "road around the park." Percival P. Baxter wanted his park to have only that road, with trails radiating from it. Off the road, he said, "you're on your own." We can bear witness that Baxter got what he wanted.

The dust-churning Perimeter Road, hardly more than a wide trail, is as plain as its name. It has not been made pretty or straight. There are no scenic overlooks. At the speed limit of 20 miles an hour, an automobile drive along the full length of Perimeter Road takes about two hours.

Nothing has ever been fancy or hurried at Baxter, including its founding. From 1917 to 1925, first as a legislator and then as governor, Percival Baxter had tried to get his state to create a park to preserve Katahdin, the glacier-sculpted crown of Maine. Since the middle of the 19th century, lumbermen had been chopping away at the forests surrounding Katahdin. Baxter feared that soon the great granite mountain would reign over a stump-marked wasteland. Even as governor, though, his had been a voice crying in Maine's wilderness.

Baxter preached preservation at a time when most people still talked of taming and exploiting the wilderness. But Baxter always believed he was right and anyone against him was wrong. He was used to shrugging at opposition. While he was governor, his dog died and he ordered the state capitol's flags lowered to half-staff. His response to public outrage was a short book, which he had printed and distributed to educate the ignorant about Man's Best Friend.

When Baxter, a wealthy bachelor, retired, he began to use his own money to buy land and build the park his state had refused to create. He envisioned a wildlife sanctuary, a Katahdin-guarded realm "where nature rules and where the creatures of the forest hold undisputed dominion."

He made his first purchase—6,000 acres centered on Katahdin—in 1930 and presented the land to the state. Parcel by parcel, he bought and deeded to Maine the forests and the mountains, the streams and the ponds that would become what he called "my park." He compared the stitching together of a park to assembling "your grandmother's patchwork quilt, which finally in some mysterious way came out of the confusion into one large piece." He sewed up the last piece in 1962, when he was 86 years old. Seven years later, he died. His ashes were scattered over what had become the fourth-largest state preserve in the nation.

Baxter State Park remains one man's legacy. The Bureau of Parks and Recreation, which administers Maine's other state parks, does not run Percival Baxter's park. State parks, he said, were "picnic grounds, with all the confusion of trailers and soda pop and all that." To make sure his park would be kept the way he wanted it, he successfully lobbied for a management separate from the state park administration. The legislature obliged by setting up the Baxter State Park Authority, which consists of Maine's attorney general, the director of the Bureau of Forestry, and the commissioner of Inland Fisheries and Wildlife. They and they alone set forth the park's regulations and policies.

For the rest of his life Baxter made the park his own. He proclaimed that nothing was to be done to interfere with nature, although he did allow hiking trails. His beloved Katahdin is the northern terminus of the Appalachian Trail. Park employees sometimes even asked his approval before clearing away trail blowdowns, which after all were nature's handiwork.

Baxter and his vision are still treated with almost religious respect. Photographs of the firm-jawed Baxter look down from the walls of park offices and ranger cabins. And when Park Director Buzz Caverly talks about the park, he often mentions "Governor Baxter" as if he were still making his rounds of the park. "Recreation is secondary here, just as Governor Baxter wanted it," Buzz told me when I asked him about the philosophy behind the park's regulations. "We take what he wanted quite seriously."

Neither aircraft nor motorboats can be used on any lake or pond wholly within park borders. At the stop-and-register gates, rangers turn away motorcycles, trail bikes, and most self-contained recreational vehicles. Radios, television sets, cassette players, and pets are also banned.

Baxter uncharacteristically bowed to local pressure and allowed hunting in certain sections of the park. He also authorized the scientific forestry area, for he believed logging need not destroy forests. His view of wilderness was a personal view, reflecting the beliefs of a man of Maine, a man whose life spanned two centuries.

In his park, hikers and backpackers could find a wilderness that tested them. And others could find a wilderness that evoked the past. Preserved in Baxter State Park, along with the woods and wildlife, was the genteel 19th-century tradition of roughing it—with the aid of a snug log cabin, a fly rod, a canoe, and a staff of cooks, waitresses, and guides.

At the turn of the century, city men went to such hideaways in Maine to get away from it all. They slept in small log cabins (called camps), ate breakfast and dinner in a central lodge, and spent the day casting trout flies into secluded ponds. The sporting camp tradition still lingered when I visited Kidney Pond Camps, then in the twilight of a life that had begun at the turn of the century. The park authority soon would close Kidney Pond Camps, to reopen it in a modern version—no dining lodge, no staff, no cook to panfry your trout for breakfast.

Percival Baxter had left Kidney Pond Camps unchanged. It had remained a place that welcomed people who wanted to outwit wild trout and people who simply want to return to their yesterdays. In recent years, however, conservationists have sought for more wilderness and less tradition. The tree-shaded camps, so quaintly perched along the shore of Kidney Pond, had become symbols of a wilderness long past.

I was a newcomer among guests who had been coming to the camps year after year for as long as half a century. Few wanted to talk about the coming end of Kidney Pond Camps. As ever, trout was the principal subject of conversation at the long dining tables.

Baxter's ponds are not stocked. The trout are wild and, by law, must be taken by fly. Surrounded by fly-rod veterans, I confessed I had never even held a fly rod. After a couple of meals at the lodge, I was apprehensive about my debut as a fly fisherman. I needed lessons. My teacher was Harry Kearney, who was beginning his 50th year as a Maine guide.

Our first trip was to the end of a wharf. I was not ready for casting from a canoe. Don't worry over being pitted against the wily trout, Harry told me. He laughed about the grave discussions he had heard concerning out-thinking wild trout. "I'm not saying I am awfully smart," he said, smiling. "But I darn well know I'm smarter than a trout."

And what about all those flies flitting through the talk in the lodge? Harry kept smiling. "If your worst problem is what fly to use," he said, "then you have to figure there isn't much stress in your life."

Next morning we were on one of the 23 ponds within four miles of the lodge. Guests signed up in advance for a pond and a cached canoe. They then paddled and hiked to their reserved pond. The system, another doomed tradition, had been designed to put one canoe in each pond.

Harry made it look easy. At the flick of his rod his line gracefully soared up and behind him, scribing a long-limbed Z in the air. Then the line lightly descended, grazing the surface in imitation of the real flies skimming around our canoe. On my first few tries, my line hastily scrawled a snarl of calligraphy and plopped into the pond, imitating a drowning fly.

"Keep your elbow in!" Harry kept saying, and I kept winging my elbow out. Finally, he placed a small stick between my elbow and my side and sternly told me not to drop the stick. It worked. I soon was casting a fly softly enough to please Harry. After more casts than I care to count, I caught my first trout, and soon my second. That night at dinner I had something to talk about.

Harry, who once was director of the park, knows almost every brook and pond. Walking with him along the trails, I remained a student. He named every wildflower and bird, read the tracks of bears and coyotes, gave me a wad of spruce gum to chew. Although he ranges much of the state as a guide, this is the place of his soul.

"Baxter is what Maine is to me," Harry said one night when he and I stopped by one of the little steep-roofed camps perched on the shore of Kidney Pond. Now and then someone put a log in the stove. I listened, the newcomer to the fire and the camaraderie, to well-honed tales.

There was another kind of wilderness here, a wilderness of memory. Harry and his two old friends spoke of a past that still was here in the warmth of the camp. Here was the time of their lives. For them, time not at Baxter was time forgotten.

"Have you seen the pond at night?" someone asked. An odd question. I had walked to their camp. I had often stood on the porch of my own camp and looked out into the night. Before I could politely answer yes, I was ushered outside and directed to a short wharf.

I stood there alone and suddenly saw what I had not seen. In the flat darkness of the pond was the dome of the sky. Stars of the heavens shone in Baxter's still waters. For a moment in that mirrored peace I was part of a night without seam, a wilderness without measure of time or space.

"Baxter
gave us
solitude,
along with
moments
that told us
we were not
alone."

20

Statuesque white-tailed doe (opposite) stops in mid-stride, ears flexed for sounds of danger. Another (below), nibbling pond plants, seems relaxed but can swiftly become an elusive swimmer. Eastern coyotes—called "brush wolves" in northern Maine—prey on the park's large deer population, mostly in winter.

FOLLOWING PAGES: Dandelion blossoms and orange hawkweed swirl around a lone apple tree in one of the few meadows found in this park of forests and peaks.

Kept by law in a "natural wild state," Baxter lives up to its mission as a "sanctuary for wild beasts and birds," including this red fox (above) peering from a cluster of bracken fern. The crystal waters of Howe Brook (opposite) rush from the green shade of yellow birch and maple. Glistening roundleaved sundew adorns a charred log (below). An insect-eating plant, the sundew attracts its prey with drops of sticky nectar. When an insect gets stuck, bristling hairlike glands curl over the victim, trapping it until the plant digests it.

Graceful white birches (opposite) screen a sun-streaked field of bracken fern and wild sarsaparilla. Birches, springing up in open spaces within Baxter's forests, provide cover for seedlings in need of shade. Browsing moose and deer savor birch twigs and leaves. Northeastern Indians, who often subsisted on sarsaparilla roots during woodland treks, used water-resistant birch bark to make canoes. Indian pipe (below) wanly nods above the forest floor. A rarity among flowering plants, Indian pipe contains no chlorophyll, and so must live off decaying vegetation. The plant's pallid appearance inspires the name ghost flower.

"Sunlight
streamed
down
on...stands
of young
white birch...
clusters
of wildflowers,
huge fans
of fern."

Reflections on Maine: Warm air draws a curtain of morning mist across mirrored beauty in Kidney Pond as eelgrass sketches its thin images. Moose twins a month or so old (opposite) sprout from a Baxter pond. People in Maine call even lake-size waters ponds. The calves, watching alertly for their mother, will stay with her for about a year, then begin life on their own. As adults, moose stand five and a half to seven feet at the shoulder and weigh 500 to 1,800 pounds, larger than any other species in the deer family.

New life thrusts from the moss-covered stump of a fire-killed pine (below). The spruce seedling must grow for about a century before it will approach the girth its host attained. Another young spruce along the Russell Pond Trail (opposite) peeks above granite boulders patched with moss. Found throughout Baxter's forests, moss holds rainwater and makes soil; rootlets attached to stone break off tiny pieces, reducing rock to dust over eons. Some 9,000 years ago an ice sheet bulldozed chunks of granite. As the glacier melted, it deposited these weathered blocks, called erratics, on slopes where trees later flourished.

Doubled in the twilight stillness of a pond, an angler lays a fly out for eastern brook trout. Yellow pond lilies (opposite) lure real insects—and hungry fish.

FOLLOWING PAGES: *New day's sun gilds tree, rock, and pond—the legacy of Baxter State Park, forever held "in Trust for . . . the people of Maine."*

"The line
lightly
descended,
grazing the
surface."

By S. Jeffrey K. Wilkerson

Photographs by David Hiser

The Last Forest
Exploring Mexico's Imperiled Lacandon Wilderness

Half airborne, a dugout ascends a travertine fall on the Tzendales River, a waterway for the author's trek through Mexico's vast Lacandon Forest.

The sudden guttural bellowing brought the tropical forest to absolute silence. Moments before, I had been peacefully guiding my dugout across one of the long dark pools of the Tzendales River, deep in Mexico's Lacandon Forest. All was tranquillity. Sunlight filtered through the immense trees, and the only noise was the incessant cadence of thousands of insects racing over the placid water.

Abruptly, the aggressive grunting was punctuated by sharp clacking, and violent thrashing erupted on the opposite bank. Standing up, I paddled cautiously across the river and nudged my craft behind some high water plants. All at once something crashed through the thorn-covered vines and the stand of bamboo on the bank. Down charged two male peccaries, hair bristling. As the chunky, piglike beasts faced each other, furiously gnashing their sharp teeth, I saw why their powerful bite is respected by all that know them—even the jungle's largest predator, the jaguar.

Such fights between competing males are common during the mating season. So preoccupied were these two that they never noticed my presence. Finally one bolted through the undercover, parting it as if he were running through soft grass. His enraged opponent followed, and the fight resumed in the distance. Peccaries have a well-earned reputation for ferocity. I was happy to be just a spectator.

I was paddling that day through a majestic rain forest on one of the most remote rivers in North America. This last great swath of primeval jungle in Mexico shelters an extraordinary array of exotic tropical flora and fauna and some of the most exquisite ruined cities of antiquity. Traveling with me were my old friend photographer David Hiser, research assistant Victoria Velasco, and an experienced field crew that had worked with me over many of my 25 years of tropical research.

We would make our way by dugout, truck, and on foot over much of the broad lowland region of the Mexican state of Chiapas. The forest, long considered an impenetrable hinterland, once stretched unbroken, eastward across Guatemala into southern Belize and northward toward the Gulf of Mexico. Most of this huge, wild area is drained by the swift-flowing Usumacinta River, which forms part of the border between Mexico and Guatemala. The lowland western portion on the Mexican bank—officially 1.48 million acres—is designated the Lacandon Forest after its few elusive human inhabitants.

They survive today, still speaking a language closely related to ancient Maya, in scattered communities near deep blue lakes in the forest. Never numerous, they now total a few hundred, and their lifestyle is changing as the once vast forest that was named for them is reduced by settlements and development projects. A very few continue their essentially pre-Columbian religious rites and wear the white-cotton, ankle-length garments of tradition. Others have opted for Christian faiths and modern western clothes.

Almost all, however, still harbor an ageless affection for the forest and its denizens. As Joaquin Trujillo Marquez, living near the village of Lacanjá, puts it, "Once it was all one land." The Lacandon may be few, and the changes in the wilderness many, but in their hearts they know that the forest still is theirs.

The town of Palenque, founded by Spanish friars in the 16th century, is the principal entrance to the forest. About thirty years ago, when my friend Moisés Morales first arrived here, the town and the Maya ruins nearby were still well within the limits of the forest. In the jungle then, he remembers with some nostalgia, "there were so many mysteries and so many incredible things that I liked to go see if it was certain the Lacandons, the chicle gatherers, and similar things that did not seem believable, might actually exist." The forest, then as now, conceals many wonders.

Today the pavement ends near Palenque. A dirt and gravel roadway, now under construction, will loop for some 300 miles around much of the forest and join isolated settlements, lumber mills, oil fields, park areas, and projected dam sites. Although many changes are afoot in this extensive region, some efforts have been made to set aside areas for the future. Besides the archaeological parks, with their somewhat limited public facilities, there is the 559,400-acre reserve of Montes Azules.

Most of this rugged wilderness is a refuge for the flora and fauna of the Lacandon Forest. Some portions have been lumbered, but the reserve, when I last saw it, still had a pristine allure. There were no roads, no settlements, and no services. One traveled only by official permission. There were few trails, and so access was mostly by river, the oldest highway of all. It was a true jungle fastness, definitely not for the casual backpacker. Rain forests are not hospitable habitats for the uninitiated.

To observe closely the grandeur of the reserve we loaded our vehicles in Palenque and followed the tortuous road into the forest. It was the height of the spring dry season. In the searing heat—we recorded up to 108°F—it took us a full day to cover the 150 miles to road's end. During the rainy season the same trip could have taken many days.

The fine limestone dust from the roadway, combined with the stifling burnoff from the newly cleared fields, kept us choking and the engine filters clogged. We camped near the wide Lacantún River and bathed away the caked dust in the clear water.

Farther on, at the village of Pico de Oro, once a lumber camp, we added Demesio to our crew. A former chicle gatherer, he is one of the last of those intrepid individuals who spent months deep in the jungle, tapping the white sap of the sapodilla tree. His profession is no more; synthetic chicle has replaced the natural ingredient in chewing gum. The chicle trails he once roamed are long since grown over. But his knowledge of the river network made him a valuable member of our crew.

Bob Grusy, a white-water expert, supervised the loading of our heavy-duty rubber raft and dugouts. Many types of boats ply the Lacantún, but experience had shown us that dugouts are the best for the obstacle-filled tributaries. After exploring the waters upstream, we chose a site at the juncture of the Tzendales and San Pedro rivers as the base camp for our examination of Montes Azules and the surrounding area.

And an excellent dry season camp it was. A strangler fig tree 110 feet tall provided much of the shade. Wild cacao and laurel were abundant. A natural palisade of thorn-covered bamboo surrounded the site. David and I laid out the camp while Demesio tended to our small flotilla. Vicki and the rest of the crew took up camp tasks. Young Doug Carlson, the newest member of our team, raked back the leaf cover as a precaution against snakes, scorpions, and other creatures that one prefers to see at a distance. Genaro Domínguez located a fragment of a large termite nest which, when burned at night in the Indian fashion, serves to repel mosquitoes. Julio Lagunes built camp tables and benches from assorted wood scrap, and former cowboy Bill Ellzey roped the tents into place.

Topography in the tropics, particularly in limestone areas, can take on odd, even fantastic configurations. Our camp was astride one of these, for the two rivers did not come together in the customary Y pattern. Instead, they flowed exactly head-on into each other before joining and then turning 90 degrees toward the Lacantún.

At first we thought that the camp would make an excellent spot for evening bathing. But soon the sighting of several large river crocodiles led us to designate a more distant spot on an island. Then the crocodiles started appearing there. Since these creatures have a less than admirable reputation, I decided that swimming would have to be a carefully planned activity with appropriate reptilian countermeasures. Everyone was required to note all daily sightings on a diagram of the river posted in camp. The evening's bathing spot was then selected from the "clear" areas.

We also found that the crocodiles would usually flee from the noise of outboard motors. Bob was assigned to use the raft like a minesweeper. After a number of roaring passes, with everyone ashore watching the water, the bathing party would be ferried to the chosen location. Baths were then taken in shallow areas of strong current under the eyes of lookouts. Perhaps the crocodiles were just curious, but given their legendary appetites, I wasn't going to let anyone test that hypothesis.

Later we were to see some large specimens upstream. For years I had heard local stories of the occasional prodigious size of the river crocodiles in this forest. In fact, alarmed settlers in one river hamlet assured David and me that a 20-foot-long "monster" lurked just around the bend. We were skeptical until I talked with Don Miguel Alvarez del Toro, Mexico's distinguished naturalist and the leading authority on Lacandon Forest fauna. He said the crocodiles can reach 23 feet in length and that when they are hungry they may be "voracious and attack all beings that come within their reach, including man."

From camp I set out one day in a small dugout to explore the lower reaches of the San Pedro. A dugout handles like no other boat. While knowledgeable sailors will tell you wood, steel, and fiberglass hulls all have differing properties, few can describe the variations in dugout design. The dying art of dugout building survives primarily in isolated tropical forests.

Maya ruins, lush flora, exotic fauna, and river-laced terrain characterize the Lacandon region—North America's last great swath of tropical rain forest. From below the gateway town of Palenque, its 1.48 million acres spread southeast to Mexico's border with Guatemala. Oil exploration, hydroelectric dams, road construction, and cattle ranching threaten this rapidly diminishing wilderness.

To Francisco Escárcega,
140 km, 87 mi

Balancán

To Villahermosa,
105 km, 65 mi

Emiliano
Zapata

Tenosique

Palenque
PALENQUE

500

1000

To Tuxtla Gutiérrez,
195 km, 121 mi

1000

CAMPECHE
TABASCO

MEXICO
GUATEMALA

TABASCO
CHIAPAS

1000

500

1000

GUATEMALA
MEXICO

4000

4000

2000

4000

2000

TONINÁ

2000

Usumacinta

YAXCHILÁN

River

1000

3000

Perlas

River

Lacanjá

BONAMPAK

Traconeja

4000

4000

3000

River

Jataté

L A C A N D O N   F O R E S T

San
Pedro

Lacanjá

5000

5000

2000

Negro

River

River

MONTES

AZULES

RESERVE

1000

River

River

Lake
Miramar

6000

Santo

Domingo

4000

River

3000

San Roman
(abandoned)

Pico de Oro

MARQUÉS
DE COMILLAS
ZONE

6000

2000

LAGUNAS DE
MONTEBELLO
NAT. PARK

Tziendales R.

Arroyo Azul

Lacantún

To Tuxtla Gutiérrez,
180 km, 112 mi

4000

MEXICO
GUATEMALA

1000

■ Maya ruin   ▌ Potential damsite

5000

0   25 km

0   15 mi

To Tapachula,
175 km, 109 mi

3000

4000

8000

9000

6000

ELEVATIONS IN FEET
CONTOUR INTERVAL 1000 FT
SUPPLEMENTARY CONTOUR AT 500 FT

Timeless continuity was on my mind while I glided along. As soon as I found the balance point I could paddle seated or standing up, weave around obstructions, or just float with the current. The trip was an experience in silent observation. No noisy ripple disturbed the surface. It was as if this hollow tree and I were a part of the river itself. No wonder the Lacandon were famous hunters. Stalking silently in a dugout, they could stealthily approach almost any prey.

Rounding bends, I saw the black shapes of great curassows, and ocellated turkeys foraging beneath the thorn thickets of the banks. They barely made an effort to move off as I passed. Iguanas sunned themselves on limbs, a crocodile languidly dropped off a log into the depths, and large white-winged ducks sped out of the way at the last possible second.

The forest was alive with the buzzing of insects and the calls of birds. Brilliant scarlet macaws and small flocks of white-fronted parrots screeched overhead. The water, having passed over mile after mile of limestone, was exceptionally clear. In the blue-green depths brightly patterned fish—some perhaps four feet long—darted about. In the ooze of the bottom lay trunks of trees that had sunk because their hard wood was denser than water.

The voyage on this crystalline river was a tranquil glimpse of a wild and secluded place. I knew that in the rainy season this same stream becomes a violent, unrestrained torrent. But today it was at peace with itself, and its hidden wonders were on display for me alone.

Another afternoon, resting during a hike in the forest, I lay on a rubber poncho and looked straight up at the colorful, many-tiered universe that spread above me. Several zones of vegetation were readily discernible in what is popularly called the jungle.

I could see all the way to the top of a nearby tree, which I later measured and found to be 135 feet tall. Macaws stopped here and briefly squabbled before flying on. Beneath this emergent giant of the first layer were the largely interlocked canopies of most of the adult trees. Many of their limbs were draped with orchids and bromeliads. From these heights a troop of howler monkeys challenged me with loud barklike calls, then settled back to eat some of the tasty, rough-skinned sapodilla fruit. Bright long-beaked toucans sampled berries in a neighboring fig tree.

The next zones contained the smaller trees, mostly immature, as well as numerous shrubs. Vanilla and other light-seeking vines grasped the trunks. A bright-green hummingbird fed on nectar from one of the white flowering allspice trees, and small black stingless bees swarmed about the minuscule entrance to their nest in a hollow limb.

The forest floor consisted mostly of moist leaves and rotting wood, out of which poked a few shade plants. The massive buttress roots of some trees gave them the look of Gothic columns; others had trunks elevated on clusters of stiltlike roots. Iridescent blue butterflies and brightly colored insects flitted about through the occasional spots of sunlight. A foraging agouti, a rodent the size of a house cat, pranced by on delicate feet in its energetic search for fallen fruit.

The major layers—emergent, canopy, lower tree, woody shrubs, floor—represent essentially the principal zones of one of the most prolific environments on earth. In a square mile of such rain forests scientists have found more than 1,000 species of flora. Most of the plants, many with potential scientific or commercial value, have never been fully studied. Even some of the animals are little known. Alvarez del Toro has shown me recently discovered creatures at the tropical-habitat zoo he directs in Tuxtla Gutiérrez, the capital of Chiapas. One was a red parrot that may belong to a new species; the other is the first armadillo of its kind ever found in Mexico. A frontier of knowledge still lies hidden in the rain forest.

Although amazingly diverse and mammoth, the forest is not fast growing. A rain forest's full growth cycle is about 400 years. When one of the giants falls or is cut, the filling in of the gap is a slow process. My crew and I once measured a mahogany tree that had been marked for cutting. It was 40 feet around just above its buttresses. How many years of history had it seen, I wondered? The man who cut it, or even his grandchildren, would never in their lifetimes see a full-size replacement.

A cloud suddenly obscured the patch of sky far above me and it started to rain, as it can do even in the February to May "dry season." As the drops filtered down through the thousands of leaves above me, I was directly reminded that water is the key ingredient in the Lacandon Forest. It receives yearly between 100 and 200 inches of rainfall, well within the margins of 80 to 440 inches for such forests worldwide. Most rain falls in the June to January "wet season," but no month is ever totally dry.

So much water falls that many plants have evolved "drip tips" on the ends of their leaves. These slender projections promote the rapid runoff of water and allow the leaf surface to dry faster. This constant moisture, along with the high tropical temperatures and the extremely efficient recycling system, allow the rain forest to sustain a colossal amount of vegetation on generally inhospitable soils. Although the forest has a towering framework, the root structure is shallow, meandering about in the narrow layer of rotting vegetation of the floor and penetrating only slightly the usually thin, rocky soils beneath.

Near the riverbank on my trek through the downpour I saw some huge overturned trees, victims of a windstorm. Their closely webbed roots seemed more like the flat bases of chess pieces than the penetrating supports one might imagine as anchors of such mighty giants. But, living on the nutrients drawn from rotting leaves and wood on the ground, the trees are part of a forest feeding endlessly upon itself, its life-sustaining wealth largely visible and vibrant.

The Tzendales, like every river in this forest, has its own flavor and runs at the heart of its own realm. To explore this wild river we started up it with a fleet of three dugouts and a rubber raft, all equipped with strong outboards. The largest dugout, piloted by Demesio, was 45 feet long.

This is no river for novices. It does not easily forgive unheeded warnings or careless behavior. The river flows rapidly almost from the beginning. Shallows with jutting rock banks are littered with tree trunks, some more than 100 feet long. They are stranded at the end of the rainy season and greatly hinder passage. Frequently we would all get out and pull our crafts through the tangled debris.

Sometimes the river would make a sharp turn and flow in rocky channels around many small wooded islands. A portage or pull through one of these treacherous passageways can be perilous. As we were struggling up one cascade, Demesio casually remarked, "One of my companions nearly drowned right here ten years ago and we all turned back."

We had to establish methodical safety procedures for each pull-up. The rocky shallow areas gave way to travertine falls that varied from a few inches to 15 feet high. These travertine formations are typical of limestone areas, particularly in the tropics, where calcium carbonate forms around rocks, logs, or other obstacles. Near these damlike structures we frequently measured pools that were 20 feet deep or more.

We were now in what is known as the "Desert of the Tzendales," a large depopulated area of dense jungle and swamp. Around the turn of the century, mahogany cutters—often debtors working as virtual prisoners—considered escape from this savage region impossible. Here we found ourselves on a long calm stretch of deep river with stout vines hanging down from tall trees whose tops nearly closed over us. The river was as dark and still as the forest around us.

At dusk we camped on an island. Soon our lanterns and campfire attracted toads of often surprising size and strength that fed on the swarms of insects around the lights. The oversize amphibians hopped about totally unconcerned with us as they feasted on their unexpected bonanza.

It had been an exhausting day, and most of the party turned in early. As I headed for my tent, Vicki matter-of-factly remarked, "A snake just crawled over my boots as I was taking them off. It was banded like a coral."

An immediate search yielded a two-foot "spotted nose." Although in the dim light it did look like a poisonous coral, this bright-colored snake is an inoffensive burrower through the leaf mulch of the forest floor. Not totally convinced, Vicki commanded: "Release it away from camp!" As jungle tradition dictates, we christened the site "Snake Island."

Early in the morning, with the humidity registering 96 percent and the temperature already 80°F, we continued upstream. Almost at once we encountered the highest fall we had yet seen. Although our equipment got through quite dry, all of us were drenched and fatigued from pulling the dugouts up over the multileveled precipice in the dangerous current.

Soon we passed more dense areas of forest, some with numerous animal trails leading down into the water. Here we searched for San Roman, the most famous of the mahogany *monterías,* or main lumber camps. Explorer Enrique Juan Palacios calculated in 1926, during the height of the first lumber boom, that in 40 years nearly 500,000 felled mahogany trees floated to market through the Usumacinta River network. Most came from the Lacandon Forest, where oxen hauled the logs to the rivers. The flooding in the wet season swept the logs downstream to sorting centers and ships waiting in the Gulf of Mexico. Palacios noted that around San Roman "the wood is more compact and finer. Its quality is superior."

We split the crew into search parties and after much effort located the camp on a thickly wooded bluff. When we began the reconnaissance of the ruins beneath the great trees, we discovered that San Roman was not merely a simple camp of convenience. The major structures were of brick and once had tile roofs. The main building, divided into many interior compartments and corridors, was more than 250 feet long. Nearby was an open-sided building, perhaps for oxen; it was more than 130 feet in length. These were impressive constructions to be undertaken in a region of extreme isolation. Clearly, fine mahogany was a fine motivator.

But today the mahogany camp is wilderness once more. Giant strangler fig trees weave their web of roots on the crumbling walls, and termites have consumed all the beams. Tapirs, primeval-looking creatures with trunklike noses, amble about in the rooms. So unaccustomed to people have these normally nocturnal creatures become that here they freely move about during the day. They are highly compact animals that can stand three and a half feet tall and weigh up to 800 pounds. Although extremely strong, these water-loving herbivores are favorite prey of jaguars.

A tapir swam among our dugouts before it realized it was being watched. Moving quickly for shore, it bolted up a pathway—and straight into our camp. The startled tapir suddenly stopped not six feet from Vicki and, being nearsighted, raised its flexible nose to inspect the unexpected tents. Now totally alarmed, it charged off, crashing through the undergrowth of the forest. Vicki, unperturbed as always, simply observed, "Next time no one puts a tent in *his* path."

One of our objectives was to reach the upper tributaries of the river, and after traversing many falls we found the Negro and Arroyo Azul. This far into the dry season, both carried very little water. But where navigation stops is a judgment call on such tropical rivers. It all depends on when you wish to stop hauling your boats up over the sharp travertine falls. Another factor for us involved our crew; two now had high fevers. So as not to take chances, we started back downriver.

On our return voyage we camped once more on Snake Island. All was as we had left it, except for tracks on top of our buried firepit. They belonged to a large feline, probably a jaguar. Curiosity aroused, the cat had visited our campsite in the brief interval that we had been upstream. How did it get there? Had it swum, as jungle cats are known to do?

Genaro and I examined the periphery of the island and encountered a previously unnoticed natural bridge to the riverbank. On the fallen trunk were the unmistakable signs of frequent crossings. It seemed that we had unknowingly been visiting the cat—and not vice versa.

Back in our main camp by the colliding rivers, we continued our exploring. On one expedition David and I were watching howler monkeys when a large gray bird swooped toward a juvenile alone on an exposed limb. The troop roared a warning, and the prospective victim barely scrambled away in time. As the bird soared off, we were left wondering about the drama a hundred feet above us. One of only two birds in the world known to attack monkeys is the harpy eagle, and there still may be a few in the Lacandon. A robust, stern-faced predator, the rare harpy is the largest eagle in the world, with a three-foot body and massive talons.

The harpy is one of the endangered species indigenous to the Lacandon. The forest also shelters magnificent treasures of the past. Hidden beneath the high canopy of the trees are hundreds of ruins. Some, such as

Yaxchilán, Bonampak, and Palenque, are impressive cities embellished with the intricate art of the Maya Classic period (about A.D. 250 to 900). Countless others are of more modest size. The abundant hieroglyphic inscriptions found at many sites bear eloquent witness to the intellectual grandeur of a literate, expressive civilization.

When the Lacandon took refuge in the forest, the earlier inhabitants had mostly abandoned their towns and fields to the forest. In a sense the Lacandon became the caretakers of the ornate vestiges of the past. Even though they did not fully comprehend their predecessors they recognized their greatness and considered their jungle-shrouded cities holy.

The Lacandon still occasionally visit a Yaxchilán temple built on a steep slope by an eighth-century ruler named Bird Jaguar. There, in the dank interior inhabited by bats, they light candles on the floor near a large sculpture fragment. The visits are less frequent now as the old beliefs fade.

On our return to Palenque from the jungle, we were able to observe the devastation of a wilderness. Just during the month we had spent traveling in the reserve, thousands of acres of forest in the adjoining region, known as the Marqués de Comillas Zone, had been intentionally burned to create fields and cattle pastures. Along the road we saw huge stands of forest in flames and some surviving jungle animals being offered for sale. The smoke from these and countless other fires formed a man-made haze covering hundreds of square miles.

As we slowly traveled the road in the swirling dust, we were passed by trucks carrying oil rigs, buses with new settlers, and logging vehicles with mahogany trunks 50 feet long. It was a panorama far different from the inspiring grandeur we had experienced in the deep forest.

We stopped to talk with my Lacandon friend Joaquin. "We were once masters of the forest," he said with pride. Then, with a tone of bewilderment, he continued: "Now all has changed. The forest was once clean, with food at hand, but if people do not conserve it there will be nothing."

His words were very much in our thoughts as we traveled onward. The heritage of millennia is harbored in the rain forest, but its useful secrets can only be unlocked by preserving it for the future. A start has been made in the archaeological parks and in the Montes Azules Reserve. Yet much remains to be done if this diverse tropical habitat is to continue to exist.

The timeless majesty of the secluded forest is haunting for all who contemplate it. None feel this more than the Lacandon. In their creation myth, the gods make the land—but at first not well: "The earth was not firm; there was no forest; there were no rocks." The deities discussed the problem, then threw sand to make stones and created the forest. "With the forest made, all was in its correct order. Then the earth was good."

Dawn mist engulfs a handmade tropical-cedar canoe poled through the placid waters of the Usumacinta River. Fed by a labyrinth of waterways, the Usumacinta links isolated settlements served by few roads. Clearing the way for farms, people increasingly replace natural haze with the murk of burnoff, at times so severe it blinds planes flying at 8,000 feet and closes airports 100 miles away.

Glaring from its perch, a harpy eagle displays the piercing eyes of a bird of prey. The Lacandon lists the harpy, which has a nearly eight-foot wingspread, among endangered animals rarely sighted in natural habitats. The yellow-necked toucan (below) resides at Mexico's renowned Miguel Alvarez del Toro Zoo, near the forest. A blooming jasmine (bottom) accents a bank of the Tzendales.

"Bright
long-beaked
toucans....
A robust,
stern-faced
predator."

Catch of the day becomes the evening's fare for the explorers, who sometimes relied on the fishing skill of Don Julio Lagunes (opposite) for their meals. He proudly shows off perch and gar. A peaceful clearing midway up the Tzendales (below) served as a camp, dubbed "Snake Island" after a colorful resident.

FOLLOWING PAGES: Author and party seek the shade of a multitrunked strangler fig for a midday rest. From treetop seedlings, figs expand outward and downward, killing their host by depriving the tree of light and strangling it.

"Perhaps the crocodiles were just curious, but..."

Peaceful pose of a river crocodile surfacing in a murky marsh (below) belies its aggressive nature. One of the last refuges for vanishing American crocodiles, the Lacandon also sustains the smaller and less feared swamp species. Signs of river crocodiles came most frequently during the search for the ruins of San Roman, a turn-of-the-century lumber camp. Confronted by impenetrable vegetation (opposite), photographer David Hiser, on a raft, and the author study maps before splitting the group into search teams that found San Roman.

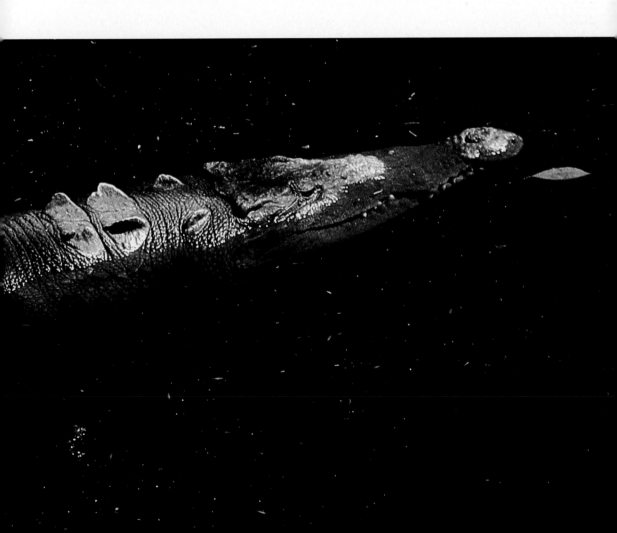

Its entryway shrouded by fast-growing roots (opposite), San Roman succumbs to the grip of the jungle. "Like a hellish end of the earth," the author said of the mahogany camp's site in the heart of the "Desert of the Tzendales." Indentured servants, virtual prisoners forced to log, learned jungle lore to survive. Juice of the water vine, for instance, quenches thirst, as Don Julio shows Vicki Velasco (below). A wary eye remains the best defense against the tarantula's irritating bite. A male (below, right), found by David Hiser, surprised him by molting under a tent flap. The shedding of the exoskeleton takes more than an hour.

Draping its nearly six-foot-long body between branches, a slender bejuquillo *(opposite) awaits prey. Fangs in the rear of its mouth prevent the snake from releasing venom until it chews. The nocturnal* mico de noche, *or* kinkajou *(below), climbs with the aid of a prehensile tail about as long as its 20-inch body.*

FOLLOWING PAGES: *Homeward-bound author and crew apprehensively look for a fall's V notch, sign of a safe path through the Tzendales' perilous waters.*

By Scott Thybony

Photographs by Tom Bean

Hidden Canyon

Trekking through Time in Utah's Grand Gulch

Grand Gulch cuts deep into the high plateau country of southeastern Utah. The winding gorge leads hikers into a cliff-hidden archaeological wilderness.

A few strokes on the oars brought the raft against a low cliff at the mouth of Grand Gulch. The boatman grabbed the bow line and climbed to a ledge halfway between the San Juan River and the perched floor of the canyon. Next to him a narrow tongue of water slid over the lip of the cliff and splashed into the river—a good sign. We would have water for the days ahead.

Water has left its imprint on this dry corner of southeastern Utah. Cutting almost a thousand feet deep into scalp-white sandstone, water has carved a canyon that twists like an old scar across the juniper-covered tablelands. Only a handful of rangers live year-round on the 500 square miles of mesa that surround the Grand Gulch Primitive Area. The rest is wilderness.

We planned to spend a week covering the 54 miles from the river to the rim of Grand Gulch and exploring the ruins of a people who had abandoned the region seven centuries before. No one knows why these Indians left their canyon homes. All that is known is that they shut their cliffside doors and never returned.

Many of the alcoves and ledges they once inhabited remain in an uncanny state of preservation. Small piles of corncobs lie stored in granaries. Underground ceremonial chambers called kivas are still intact. Soot-smudged walls hold the impressions of fingers left when the mud plaster was smoothed by hand, and vividly painted figures of humans and animals march along cliff faces.

The other raft tied up, and we began unloading wet bags packed with trail gear. The ledge was soon crowded with four of us sorting through piles of clothes and food. Stewart Aitchison, occasional guide and full-time naturalist, was an old hand at dividing up the food. He made sure that Buck Crowley got the ten-pound jar of peanut butter. This was Buck's first backpacking trip, so he didn't care how much weight he carried as long as it was food. Tom Bean, photographer and former park ranger, looked at the growing pile of camera gear in front of him and shook his head.

The river guides cleared a spot to fix breakfast. To get a fast start, we had left our riverside camp at first light without bothering to eat, then floated down an early morning San Juan as smooth and dark as obsidian.

It had taken us three days on the river just to reach the jump-off point for Grand Gulch. We had put in on the San Juan at the small town of Mexican Hat. Below the town the river runs fast and broken, winding through a series of deep horseshoe bends called the Goosenecks. On the way downriver we had camped at two remote canyons that drain the high plateau. One night rain had moved in as we set up camp. Heavy, rolling thunder had echoed down the canyon.

Now, in fine weather, we stood at the mouth of Grand Gulch watching the guides row into the main current. The rafts drifted away, leaving us with only one way to go—up and out.

As Buck hefted his heavy pack over a shoulder, a gush of water burst from the top. He had forgotten to tighten the lid on his canteen. While he opened his pack to inspect the damage, Tom offered some wry advice: "It works better if you screw the top on first."

It felt good to be on our own and walking into new country. Ahead, the canyon walls rose like two bookends supporting nothing but a band of blue sky. The gorge soon narrowed into a choke point jumbled with boulders and slump blocks—large chunks of fallen stone. There was no direct way to proceed. Under heavy packs we detoured, scrambled, and backtracked. No one could keep a steady pace.

We were heavily loaded with food for a week and several quarts of water each. Buck was carrying about 50 pounds in a borrowed pack that looked as if it had been designed for 40. He had not gone far before he realized what was in store for him. "The secret to this," he joked, "is you walk until your mind dulls, then you don't care any more." As he took a wrong turn behind a boulder, I heard his voice trailing off: "Don't worry, it's agony for two or three days. Then it's just hell."

Buck wasn't alone. Everyone was paying the price for being away from the backcountry too long. The routine of walking felt awkward and stiff. We had to think through simple things like choosing the best route and the right pace to walk. But in spite of our preoccupation with putting one foot in front of the other, we kept scanning the walls ahead for any signs of prehistoric ruins left by the Anasazi, ancestors of today's Pueblo Indians.

Before we started the trip I had heard a rumor of a remarkable kiva that only a few people knew about. It was supposed to be so undisturbed that its roof was intact and the original ladder still rested inside the smokehole. In Arizona and New Mexico, Pueblo tribes, including the Hopi, use kivas for religious activities and as a social gathering place for the men of the tribe. Hopi say that old abandoned kivas are important to them and should be treated with respect. One Hopi told me I could enter the ruins of a kiva—but I might want to leave a pinch of bread for the spirits of the dead.

Although many sites in Grand Gulch are well preserved, I could not believe that among them was a kiva that had remained practically unknown after a hundred years of looters and enthusiastic archaeologists. But I kept my eyes open.

During a hike one day, I noticed a set of boot tracks. Something looked odd about them. The tracks dropped off a slickrock slope and crossed a patch of undisturbed soil. I could not see any reason for tracks to be there—no water, no ruins, no unusual scenery, not even a pretty flower. Someone, purposely taking a roundabout way, had tried not to leave a direct trail. It might lead to the hidden kiva.

I left my pack and scrambled up the talus slope to the base of the canyon wall. Pushing through brush, I followed along the cliff. The rock flared outward in a protective overhang hundreds of feet thick. Great chunks of fallen sandstone littered the foot of the cliff.

I worked my way into a cavernous alcove where the harsh light of midday was softened by the enveloping rock. Everything was still. Nothing moved. No sound filtered in. The rock chamber was like a great empty cathedral waiting to be filled.

Climbing a boulder, I saw nothing but more broken rock. So I kept on walking. The floor leveled off. A couple of potsherds lay on a rock. I looked ahead through a gap between the boulders. Two long wooden poles jutted from the floor. It was a kiva.

I ran toward it, each stride echoing through the rock chamber like a drumbeat. Usually I approach a site slowly and carefully, studying the ground for clues that others have overlooked. This time I kept running.

I had never seen anything like it. The kiva was large, roughly 20 feet by 20 feet. A low stone wall supported a dirt-covered roof that camouflaged the structure, making it difficult to tell where archaeology ended and geology began. The only way into the ceremonial room was through a square smokehole in the roof, where the ends of the ladder emerged.

Except for the rungs that had fallen off the ladder, everything was in perfect condition, nearly undisturbed for at least 700 years. There was a remarkable similarity between this kiva and those still in use on the Hopi mesas. To call it a ruin would be misleading. Nothing had collapsed, nothing had weathered. I ran my hand along the corner of the wall, touching the hard edge of the unburied past.

Kivas were usually built next to the homes of Pueblo Indians. This one stood alone, a sanctuary placed far away from other structures. Removed from its surroundings, the underground chamber would be an archaeological curiosity. But here, in place and undisturbed, it had a powerful presence. It was located in a spot perfectly balanced with its surroundings. From the angle where I stood, the white edge of the sandstone ceiling cut a sharp parabolic curve against the blue sky. The tapered ladder poles bisected the curve, forming a bridge between rock and sky.

Concerned about possible damage, I stayed off the roof. I leaned over and looked through the smokehole. There were no tracks in the thick dust of the floor. I wanted to drop through the smokehole, but I knew that curiosity might destroy what I hoped to discover. The risk of damaging the ladder or the roof was too great. I headed back, leaving the kiva undisturbed.

Grand Gulch is a vertical world. Huge slab walls rise from a splayed slickrock foundation. Hard rains and flash floods have chiseled towering pinnacles and deep alcoves. Beds of red shale finger their way through canyon walls of white sandstone. The softer shale weathers faster than the sandstone, which sometimes forms overhangs. Where water has dripped over the sandstone rim, streaks of iron or manganese oxides—desert varnish—blacken the cliff.

We followed the stream as it pooled up in shallow basins, sank beneath gravelly stretches, then reappeared over smooth rock beds. Runoff from the winter snows in the high country had found its way into the canyon. In dry weather only the spring-fed portions continue to flow, until the floods come. Piles of driftwood mark where high water had pounded and churned its way through the canyon. Two months' rain can fall in a single downpour. Since bare rock, rather than vegetation, covers most of the rim country, much of the rain is quickly funneled into the deep canyons.

We stopped to rest in a pocket of shade at the base of an undercut cliff.

Three steep-walled Utah canyons dissect the high tablelands of Polly and Cedar mesas. Grand Gulch, Slickhorn Canyon, and Johns Canyon drain into the deeply entrenched San Juan River. A Bureau of Land Management Primitive Area, Grand Gulch drops about 3,000 feet along its 54-mile course.

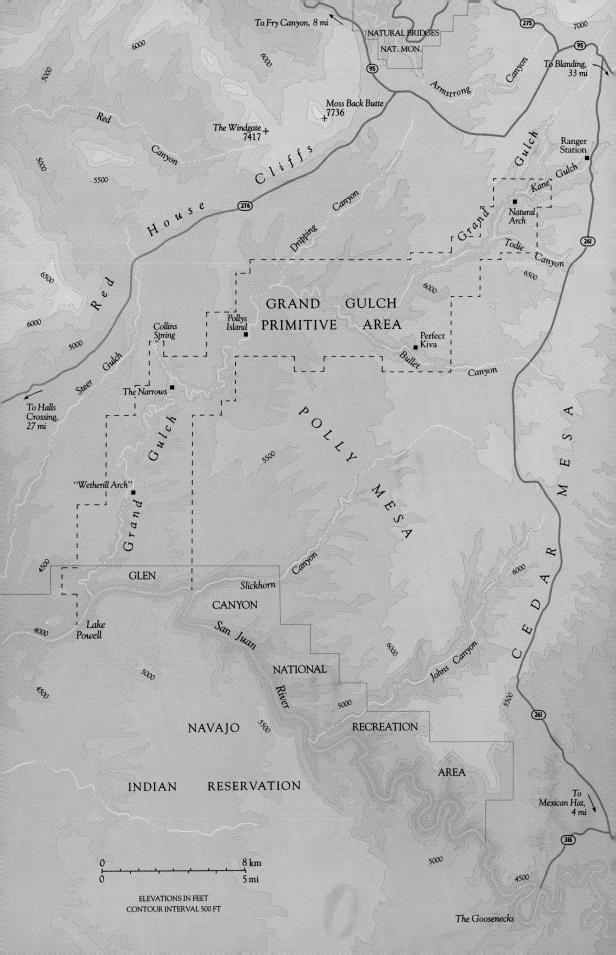

To Fry Canyon, 8 mi

NATURAL BRIDGES
NAT. MON.

275

7000

95

To Blanding,
33 mi

Armstrong

Canyon

6000

6000

Moss Back Butte
7736

The Windgate
7417

Red

5000

5000

Canyon

5500

House

Cliffs

276

Dripping

Canyon

Grand

Gulch

Ranger
Station

Kane

Gulch

Natural
Arch

Todie

Canyon

261

6500

6000

6500

6500

GRAND   GULCH
PRIMITIVE   AREA

6000

6000

Red

Collins
Spring

Pollys
Island

Perfect
Kiva

Steer

Gulch

5000

The Narrows

Bullet

Canyon

To Halls
Crossing,
27 mi

POLLY

MESA

"Wetherill Arch"

Grand

Gulch

5500

MESA

CEDAR

6000

4500

GLEN

Canyon

Slickhorn

4000

Lake
Powell

CANYON

San Juan

6000

Johns Canyon

5000

4500

5000

River

NATIONAL

5000

261

NAVAJO

5500

RECREATION

AREA

INDIAN   RESERVATION

To
Mexican Hat,
4 mi

316

5000

4500

0   8 km

0   5 mi

ELEVATIONS IN FEET
CONTOUR INTERVAL 500 FT

The Goosenecks

High above, a pair of white-throated swifts tumbled through the air, courting on the wing. These acrobatic birds seem to do everything at full throttle, catching insects without slowing down and even scooping water in full flight. Another swift shot in front of us on a kamikaze course straight for the cliff. It disappeared. I walked over to take a closer look. What I thought was solid rock was split by a narrow crevice. Deep inside, the bird had built a nest.

The map indicated a natural arch about seven miles from the river. It was late in the day by the time we reached it. The arch was massive, more a hole punched through the base of the canyon wall than a graceful span. The arch apparently had been created by floods that had scoured the narrow neck of a meander until it had thinned enough to break through. Great blocks of sandstone had fallen beneath the span. In between these, the ground was level enough for sleeping. The arch had sheltered travelers since prehistoric times. We followed their lead and stopped for the night.

On the ground around our campsite we saw prehistoric corncobs and bits of yucca string. Someone had carved the name "Wetherill Arch" on a log near camp. Our map had not given the place an official name, but that would be a good choice. Richard Wetherill was a seasoned guide, rancher, and self-taught archaeologist. After discovering the major cliff dwellings at Mesa Verde, Colorado, he led several expeditions into Grand Gulch in the 1890s and excavated many of the ruins.

He took his new bride, Marietta, on a winter collecting trip. Before long their camp overflowed with woven robes, sandals, pots, beautiful baskets, and mummies—centuries-old burials that had been naturally desiccated by the dry climate. One night it began snowing, so Richard got up to save his finds. On his last trip back to the cave, he was dragging a mummy under each arm. "Where would you like them?" he asked his suddenly awakened wife. "At the head of the bed or at the foot?"

After lunch the next day I turned a bend and spotted a large blue man near the canyon rim. Leaving my pack behind, I pushed through the streamside thicket and headed up a talus slope. A low cliff blocked the way, but someone had propped a log against it for a makeshift ladder.

Climbing higher, I saw that the blue man was painted on a smooth wall in a dreamscape of other images. Figures—whether human or supernatural was not clear—wore elaborate headdresses and stood next to birds, a shield, and a row of feathers. A large man, perhaps a shaman, held a rattle; a cloud of symbols rose from the top of his head. Animals, people, and geometric designs overlapped each other, as if on a blackboard that had not been erased. If there was a story line here, I missed it.

Although petroglyph and pictograph panels are scattered throughout Grand Gulch, we don't know the intentions of the Indians who created them. Our distinctions between art, religion, and historical records may have meant nothing to them. The rock art may have been involved in all three. Unsure of what they represented, I found myself looking with a critical eye one moment and a sense of awe the next. Many of the paintings displayed a quirk I had not seen in other pictographs. A number of the human figures had their right arms raised, as if to wave hello or good-bye.

The last canyon dwellers in this area abandoned their homes and fields around 1275 and never returned. Yet some of the rock art may date much earlier. Indians we now call the Anasazi may have entered Grand Gulch as long as 2,000 years ago.

When Richard Wetherill excavated the canyon's cliff alcoves, he found storage chambers that were often used for burials. There was no evidence that the earliest known Anasazi had lived in these natural shelters. Their descendants elsewhere built suites of stone and adobe rooms, sometimes multistoried. Although the Anasazi hunted game and gathered such wild food as piñon nuts and grass seeds, it was corn that was essential to their way of life. Studies have shown that corn may have made up as much as 75 percent of the Anasazi diet.

People came into the region in waves. Early Anasazi lived here for 200 years, then withdrew. The region was left unoccupied for hundreds of years until the next surge of Anasazi reached the gulch. This new generation brought with them pottery, the bow and arrow, and other innovations. The greatest use of the canyon itself occurred with a third wave around 1050 and lasted until the end of the 13th century, when the entire region was abandoned for good.

Fighting among the canyon's inhabitants increased during the final years the Indians lived in Grand Gulch. Archaeologists have found evidence that they dismantled their homes and used the stone to build defensive walls. Many of these walls contain loopholes just big enough for a defender to aim and shoot an arrow through.

We camped next near the Narrows, where flowing water has cut a slot only .15 feet wide through the neck of a deep meander. A still pool of water stood in the throat of the passage, reflecting a thin blue line of sky. Even when bright sunlight covered the rest of the canyon, this pool lay in the shadow of the high walls. On a ledge nearby, six white figures stood together against the red rock. They all held hands, and two wore headdresses. One of the figures in the group appeared fainter than the others; I wondered if it depicted a child who had died. It looked like a family portrait left here between the lower and middle sections of the canyon.

Because of the standing water, the gnats were bad. We turned in early to get away from them. Not able to sleep, I thought about this strange archaeological wilderness we had entered. These winding stone corridors were like a museum turned inside out. Instead of seeing artifacts removed from their natural setting and displayed behind glass, we saw everything in place. We were the ones who had left behind our normal surroundings. Days from a paved road or phone, we had become artifacts of another time and place.

Late the next day we reached Pollys Island, a huge block of mesa stranded from the rest of the rim when the stream changed its course long ago. It was sheer-sided and looked hard to climb. Looping behind it was a large, cut-off meander called a rincon.

Leaving our packs at camp, we set out in separate directions to explore the area. It was still hot. Even the wind had been deflated by the sun and dragged itself with effort up the canyon.

69

Within the rincon and hidden from the creek, a small cliff dwelling sat in a deep socket of rock. On the lintel of the main room, the archaeologist Nels Nelson had carved his name. Nelson had led an American Museum of Natural History expedition into the gulch in 1920, retracing Wetherill's route and relocating some of his earlier excavations. Nelson, in his field report, commented on the effect that the wilderness had on civilized man: "His mind may be cleverer than ever before, and yet to judge by his own exterior he may look like a degenerate." I hadn't seen a mirror in six days, so I couldn't vouch for myself, but judging by the ragtag appearance of those around me, we were good examples.

Tom had climbed about two-thirds of the way up Pollys to a granary, a small Anasazi storage room. He thought we might be able to reach the top of the mesa if we hauled up a log to use as a ladder. Wetherill had reported small living sites on top, so we knew there had to be a way up. That night we made our plans.

We ate breakfast as the morning light shone through the new leaves of the cottonwoods, igniting them in an incandescent green. At the first cliff, we passed a log up a route where a few weathered handholds and footholds had been pecked into the rock face. At the next cliff, a pile of rocks supported a rickety juniper limb that Wetherill himself might have left behind. We propped our log alongside the limb only to find that the log barely reached the next niche in the face of the cliff.

Each of us in turn climbed the nubbins on the wobbly log as high as possible, then lunged forward and flattened against the rock. We scrambled to the next ledge just under the flared lip of the rim and found a short log to lean against the rim for the last pitch.

From the top of the mesa, the sky spread all the way to the far horizon. After spending days hemmed inside the canyon, we felt as if we had opened the door and stepped outside. As far as the eye could see, there were no roads, no houses, no wires; all the straight lines of the imagination were curved and softened. To the east, piñon and juniper trees stuck out from the rim like the hair on the back of a dog's neck. Rain clouds lifted above Moss Back and the Windgate, two distant buttes to the north. The climb to the rim had suddenly expanded the world, leaving us as exposed and cut off as the sky island we stood on.

The top was smaller than it had seemed from below. A number of collapsed walls lay under protecting rocks, and potsherds and flaked stones were scattered everywhere. I picked up a shard. Each clay coil was pinched on top of the next, producing a corrugated texture that resembled the layered walls of the canyon. The design of the hatching on another shard was as black and sharp-edged as the willow shadows I had seen cast against the white sand on the canyon floor.

The pottery fragments were not here by accident. Whoever had lived on this nearly inaccessible rock had to have containers for the food and water they carried up. A large natural basin in the rock caught some rain. But as the season warmed, the water would dry up quickly. What little soil that did exist was too shallow to farm. Why did they go to the trouble to live here? One answer seems to be fear of attack, and they may have had good reason to be afraid. Some form of violence appears to have plagued even the earliest residents of the gulch.

A number of Wetherill's mummies showed signs of sudden death. An old man nearly six feet tall, unusually large for an Anasazi, had been slashed across the back and stomach. Someone had sutured the ragged wound with a cord of braided human hair. His right hand clenched the wound; his left hand gripped the right. "The face," Wetherill wrote, "seems to indicate pain."

Days on the trail were measured, not in miles, but by events: an interesting ruin, a good spring, a fine rock-art site. Painted handprints were so common that we usually passed them by with little notice. But one wall was covered with hundreds of them in reds, blues, whites, and greens. There were so many disembodied hands that they resembled a great flock of colorful birds taking flight.

At times the clouds piled up on the rim as if they were growing straight out of the rounded, hummocky rock formations on top. Early geologists, perhaps homesick for wetter climates, gave rocks such names as toadstools, haystacks, and biscuits.

Leaving the main trail to avoid slogging through the stream, we dragged ourselves up a steep, sandy bypass onto a high terrace. Stewart decided to slosh ahead. After a hundred yards, the path we were following dead-ended at a cliff that dropped straight to the creek. We were rimrocked. Buck saw Stewart walking calmly fifty feet below. "Stewart," he shouted. "You're looking like a genius right about now." We had to backtrack to the floor of the canyon.

Since many of the cliffside living sites were built at prominent locations close to the trail, they were impossible to miss. Others were easily overlooked. From a distance, some blended so well with the canyon rock that the only hint of their presence was a black doorway that seemed to lead into the dark interior of the rock itself.

We got sidetracked for more than an hour during the heat of the afternoon trying to find a well-preserved ruin we had heard about. We finally spotted it perched on a high ledge in a side canyon. From below, the rooms resembled blocks of clay stuck in a crease of the rock.

While Buck and I checked a long vertical crack to see what was in store for us if we tried to climb, Tom found another way. We followed his route and joined him on the ledge. The centuries-old cliff dwelling was in better condition than some I had seen in Mexico still inhabited by Indians. The plastered walls looked wet to the touch. Beams, still bark-covered, were lashed with split twigs, each tied in a square knot. A bold, lime-green design spanned the outer wall of the main room.

An excavation gives you a sense of history; the deeper you dig, the older things get. But this Anasazi home was too untouched by time to evoke feelings of an ancient past. I expected the family that had lived here to return at any moment.

Although archaeologists had already surveyed the site, we were careful not to disturb what remained. A stone slab set in the entryway sealed a room, but it was obvious from the tracks and wear marks that the room had been entered in recent times. Even so, I felt a twinge of apprehension when I knelt down to remove the slab. Gently lifting the stone, I looked inside. It was cool and dark with a sour smell from generations of pack rats. My eyes took a few moments to adjust to the darkness.

The room was empty. But the quiet itself seemed tangible. It was like the silence that hangs in the night air of the desert when the living things stop and wait for me to walk by. I felt uneasy and replaced the stone.

We passed the junction with Bullet Canyon and entered the upper section of the gulch. At the gnarled roots of an old cottonwood we dropped our packs and made camp. The day pivoted into night, filling the canyon with blue shadows and soft red light. A chorus of canyon tree frogs began to serenade us from a nearby stream's deep plunge pool. It's hard to believe that a thumb-size frog can make such a large mammalian sound.

Stewart disappeared after dinner. Later, when I walked down to the pool, I saw him standing at the water's edge. The frogs had stopped croaking. "I'm waiting for the frogs to show themselves," Stewart said. He has an unusual rapport with amphibians. He wanted to meet the neighbors without spooking them into a headlong leap into the water.

The next day we hiked to within seven miles of our destination and made camp. That evening I climbed to a fold of rock overlooking the canyon floor. Tom and Stewart had followed a steep ravine to the rim. Buck was back at camp, doctoring a broken tooth.

I was surrounded by cliff walls as smooth and contoured as flesh. The slickrock was still warm from the day's sunlight. If I had felt a pulse I wouldn't have been surprised. It's as close to living stone as we'll find. The upper canyon breathed with life. Pines covered the slopes; green cottonwoods, willow, tamarisk, and box elder hugged the stream. It was a long lifeline winding through the desert — arterial, green with vegetation.

Overlooking the floor of the canyon was a brown dust-covered ruin. The life that animated it had long since gone, absorbed back into rock, water, and sky. Or so it seemed as the colors drained one by one from the evening sky. First the reds disappeared and then the yellows, leaving a deep blue twilight.

I walked back to camp, where Buck was vigorously shaking his thin sleeping bag, trying to bring back its loft. The nights were noticeably cooler here, 2,000 feet higher than the river we had left a week before. Tomorrow we would hike up and out Kane Gulch to the ranger station, where we had arranged to have someone meet us.

I told Buck he had better be careful tonight. This was the last chance for an Anasazi ghost to find him. Just as I said it, a large bird swooped out of the dark and flew over his head. He ducked, but the bird was already gone.

Weathering exposes the sinuous layers of Cedar Mesa sandstone, showing its waterborne, windswept origin. Ocean currents, 270 million years ago, deposited sand that winds reworked into coastal dunes when sea level dropped. Wind and water now turn the rock back into sand. Cedar Mesa sandstone forms not only the walls of Grand Gulch but also the surrounding plateau and the spectacular rock formations at the nearby Natural Bridges National Monument.

Floating through the shadow of cliffs 1,000 feet high, rafters on the San Juan River (below) drift toward their destination, Grand Gulch, a mile downriver. Labeled "Impassable Cañon" on early maps, the river's lower gorge was not accurately surveyed until the 1920s. Rough talus slopes reach to water's edge. Hikers (opposite) pick their way through a boulder-choked ravine at the mouth of Grand Gulch. Most of the 4,000 hikers who explore here each year remain on the more accessible upper-canyon trails near the Kane Gulch Ranger Station. The desert spiny lizard, (opposite, lower) keeps from overheating at midday by facing into the sun, exposing less of its body surface to direct light.

"Water has
carved a canyon
that twists
like an
old scar."

Sunlight appears through a rock window eroded in a narrow sandstone wall near Todie Canyon (below). When rain and melted snow drip over the cliff, minerals leach from the rock and stain the surface in dark streaks called desert varnish. Newly leafed branches of a Frémont cottonwood tree (opposite) spread in silhouette at the mouth of Todie Canyon. Cottonwoods, often found in groves, share the fertile streamside environment with box elder, tamarisk, and willow.

FOLLOWING PAGES: Storm clouds gather as a rainbow arches over Grand Gulch near its junction with Bullet Canyon, whose rim shows on the right. Because hikers at the bottom of the 600-foot gulch can see only a narrow band of sky, the fast-moving storms that lash them often come as a drenching surprise.

Perfect Kiva stands empty where Anasazi men once gathered to pray and talk about the day's events. A modern ladder (below) rests in the smokehole—the only entrance to the underground chamber. The ladder pokes through the kiva roof in front of a restored masonry room (opposite, lower). Sheltered in a large rock alcove, the site stays cool in summer shadows but is warmed by low-angle sunlight in winter. Gaping doorways (opposite, upper) reveal the location of a granary tucked away on a nearly inaccessible ledge. These structures stored food for Indians who withdrew from the region around 1275. Bureau of Land Management regulations prohibit unauthorized entry into kivas.

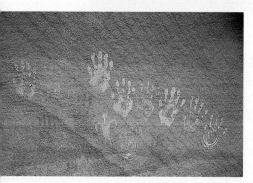

"Painted figures
of humans
and animals
march
along cliff
faces."

Painted designs decorate the walls of Green House Ruin (below), well protected by a natural rock ceiling hundreds of feet thick. Anasazi rock art reflects a vivid imagination but its meaning remains a mystery. It may record historical events or depict rituals whose significance is lost. Ghostly handprints (opposite, lower) surround a small human figure. Artists used an unusual combination of pecking and overpainting to create such works as the two figures that appear to be waving (opposite, upper) and the stylized animal that resembles a bighorn sheep (left).

"I was
surrounded
by cliff walls
as smooth
and contoured
as flesh."

Bright green cottonwoods (below) grow near an intermittent stream that creates a ribbon of life winding through the high desert. Grayish green clumps of sagebrush cover the drier terraces. Evening comes early to the Narrows (left), where churning floods over time have cut a high-walled chute 15 feet wide.

FOLLOWING PAGES: With the Red House Cliffs as a massive backdrop, Grand Gulch disappears in its own shadow as night wells up from the bottom of the canyon. At eventide the stark rim country becomes a land of rock, where the light itself becomes crystalline and the shadows stand as solid as onyx.

By Cynthia Russ Ramsay

Photographs by Michael S. Yamashita

The Great Burn

From Rockies Wildfire, a Gem of Wild Beauty

Tranquil Leo Lake reflects an idyllic campsite in the Great Burn. Snags recall fires that inspired the name of this wilderness on the Idaho-Montana border.

The remarkable thing about our campsite was not the alpine meadow radiant with flowers, not the shining lake that mirrored jagged ridges stabbing the sky. Even the memorable sightings of wildlife did not define the special character of the place, although certain images of animals add enchantment to my recollections of this high, wild country astride the Idaho-Montana border: The trio of deer returning at dusk and gazing at us with unfathomable eyes; the moose browsing in the water and bringing up mouthfuls of dripping plants; the cow elk and her calf trotting out of a thicket, pausing for a moment, as still as statues, and then melting back into the brush.

What made this landscape so dramatic were the dead trees—stark, eerie forests of them. Desiccated, stripped of most of their branches, but tenaciously upright, they studded the talus slopes and emerged from crevices on the craggy heights.

Bleached to a silvery pallor by decades of wind and weather, these snags brought an austere beauty to Leo Lake, 6,415 feet high in the midsection of the Bitterroot Range. The skeletal shapes achieved a sculptural grace in sunlight, when the wood's convoluted grain emerged in clear detail. In the wet gloom of a rainstorm, the trees became sinister apparitions looming through the mist. At all times, the strange relics were mute reminders of the great fire of 1910, when about 3 million acres of forest burned in just a few days.

From May to August of that year little rain had fallen in the Rockies of Idaho and Montana. The withered vegetation was tinder-dry. About 2,000 fires—a few caused by lightning, most by careless railroaders, homesteaders, and prospectors—plagued the region. But fire fighters managed to contain most of them with trenches. Then on August 20 gale-force winds fanned the smoldering forest floor, touching off a conflagration. Flames leaped from treetop to treetop and jumped across ravines. Only a few valleys escaped the blaze as the intense heat generated huge convection currents that whirled tornadoes of fire through the smoke-filled darkness.

Eighty-five people perished. Others trapped in the inferno lived to tell of their terrible ordeal. Some survived by taking refuge in a creek and throwing buckets of water as high as they could to drench the trees around them. Their eyewitness accounts describe the "screaming, hissing, and snapping of millions of doomed trees," the whoosh, like a Roman candle, of evergreens exploding into torches as flames raced through dry needles.

The rugged, roadless country around Leo Lake, now within the proposed Great Burn wilderness, was only one of the many areas devastated by the 1910 fire. In the Rocky Mountains nearly every square mile of forest has been repeatedly burned. Fire is as much a natural part of the ecosystem as rain. Fire clears litter from the forest floor, aids the process of decomposition, consumes diseased trees and the insects that attack them, creating light and space for new growth. And as soon as the ground is cool, the forests begin anew with such sun-loving pioneer species as lodgepole pine.

But in the proposed Great Burn wilderness, an irregularly shaped fragment carved out of the vast Lolo and Clearwater National Forests, the effects were more far-reaching because of other fires that swept through a few years later. In some areas the fires destroyed the new growth of lodgepole pines before they matured, thus killing the seed source for reforestation. Grasses and shrubs sprouted, creating large meadows. Trees were missing because of the fires, not because of elevation.

"At this latitude, tree line goes up to at least 9,000 feet, but we'll find large expanses of meadows at a much lower elevation, where, logically, trees should be," said Ken Wall, assistant director of the Wilderness Institute at the University of Montana. We were on our way from Missoula, Montana, to Leo Lake, a 2½-hour drive, mostly on dirt roads.

By the time we arrived at the trailhead, clouds had drifted down from the peaks, dissolving the wide horizons into a gray void. Shreds of mist sailed across our narrow field of vision, their rapid flow giving substance to the raw wind. A few yards from the trail the land dropped off sharply. Below us was a circle of clarity undimmed by the enveloping mist—the Irish Basin, where lush grasses registered each chill gust with rippling waves.

"That's perfect elk country because it has the cover, the food, and the marshy spots they seek," Ken said as he squinted through binoculars. "Elk are very wary animals, spooking more easily than deer. For most of the day, they bed down and hide in the timber, chewing their cud. Early in the morning and in the evening they come out to feed on sedges and grasses and to roll around in the mud wallows for protection against flies."

Though there are as many as 1,000 elk in the Great Burn in summer, we saw none. And soon we did not see the trail, which dwindled away on a bleak crest of slabby rock made bleaker still by spectral mist and snags. After we had traversed two more ridges, rain was beating a heavy tattoo on my hooded slicker; when I looked up, water trickled down my face and neck. But mostly my eyes remained fixed on my feet, for I was intent on picking my way around snags that had blown down and lay half-buried.

I also made a point of avoiding the clumps of beargrass, which, along with mountain heather, grows in great profusion in the meadows of the Great Burn. Sometimes, though, there was no place else to put my feet, so I wobbled from one slippery tussock to another.

Some beargrass was in bloom, each plant producing a solitary bulbous cluster of creamy-white tufts atop a stalk. The stalks were as tall as five feet, but even at that impressive height they were not sturdy enough to grab onto. A plant may take three to five years to produce its flower, and then, likely as not, elk come along and neatly snip it off, leaving the stem in place. A field of stems looked like a barricade set up against intruders.

For the first three hours I hiked with anticipation, assuming we would arrive in a camp with tents set up and a fire going, for photographer Mike Yamashita, his assistant Kathryn Evers, and Missoula businessman and conservationist Dale Harris were awaiting us at Leo Lake. But the rain was becoming streaked with snow, and Ken decided it made no sense to go any farther in near-zero visibility, especially since we had left behind our topographical map. We made our way back to the car by compass.

We set out again from Missoula the next day, which began deceptively sunny. We made it to camp before the breeze became a bluster and fat, gray clouds again massed on the ridges. Dale was sawing with a crosscut, Kathryn was collecting twigs, and Mike was coaxing small sputtering flames that soon became a cheerful, crackling blaze. Burning within a circle of rocks, the fire cooked supper, dried socks, provided a friendly warmth, and held our attention with a fascination that defied logical explanation.

I also enjoyed watching the procession of clouds rolling over a saddle in the skyline of sharp-cut ridges that enveloped the lake on three sides. With a rumble of thunder came a cold wind that brought a stratus of steely darkness. Then a sliver of blue slid into view, followed by a succession of fleecy white clouds. On the lake, slanting shafts of sunlight flared on the shadowy, rippling surface. Soon, fiery tints of sunset seeped across the western sky and bathed the landscape in a rosy glow.

"Up here, we can get summer and winter in the same day," said Dale. "Usually it's one hour of summer and twenty of winter."

In the course of the lingering, incandescent evening, which atoned for the previous misery, Dale spoke of his long commitment to the Great Burn, a place he had first explored in the summer of 1971 as a college student and as a participant in a wilderness project. For years he and the Great Burn Study Group have campaigned for legislation to have some 250,000 acres included in the National Wilderness Preservation System.

"I realized that the mountain goats, moose, and deer didn't have voices to represent themselves. They didn't have any control over their destiny. I felt a moral responsibility to speak in their behalf," said Dale, whose amiable, low-key manner belies his energy and determination. He has moved swiftly in local skirmishes with the U. S. Forest Service, using administrative procedures to halt road construction and logging in parcels totaling 20,000 acres within the proposed wilderness.

"When we first started," Dale said, "the feds were so eager to harvest timber that they were ready to go into unproductive steep terrain. Such ventures would ultimately have cost the taxpayers money." Dale and his group have successfully negotiated every appeal they have filed. Legislation designating the Great Burn a national wilderness has been put in the hands of Congress. Such protection would ban logging, keep out roads and motorized vehicles (including snowmobiles), and even prohibit the use of chain saws to clear trails.

We spent the next day exploring the higher elevations, hoping to see wildlife, but anticipating even more the freedom to amble along, unhurried and unencumbered by schedule or agenda, seeing what we could see. None of it was easy walking. The avalanche chutes, despite their steepness, lured us with their flowers.

Fuchsia blossoms grew in a serpentine pattern, following the meanders of a small spring that oozed out of the ground and trickled downhill. Indian paintbrush and yarrow, which grows in small, flat-topped clusters, dominated the hillside, giving it a vermilion and white tinge. Close to the

Strikingly diverse terrain—steep mountains, forested valleys, and verdant meadows—provides habitat for the Great Burn's elk, moose, black bear, mountain goat, and deer. About 100,000 acres lie in Montana's Lolo National Forest. In Idaho the land drains into Kelly Creek, famed for its cutthroat trout. The State Line Trail roughly bisects the proposed national wilderness.

To St. Regis,
23 mi

LOLO
NATIONAL
FOREST

6000

5500

6500

ST. JOE
NATIONAL
FOREST

6500

Trout Creek

6500

MONTANA
IDAHO

6000

6500

French
Lake

7500

5500

Clark

Fork

Tarkio

90

Rivulet

To
Missoula,
33 mi

5000

5000

Hoodoo Pass

BITTERROOT

6000

Heart Lake

5500

STATE

6000

LINE

5000

North

Fork

5000

Fish

Creek

LOLO

5000

North

Fork

TRAIL

Crater Mountain
7663

Straight

Creek

Hole in the Wall
Lodge

5000

Clearwater

River

6000

Straight

Straight Peak
7646

Fork

West

Chilcoot Pass

4000

5000

NATIONAL

5500

Siamese
Lakes

5000

6500

South

Fork

5000

CLEARWATER

5500

Fish
Lake

Fork

Kelly
Lake

6000

Irish
Basin

Cache

Creek

FOREST

5500

5000

STATE

LINE

5500

4000

TRAIL

Leo Lake

R

6000

6500

MONTANA
IDAHO

Kelly

Creek

NATIONAL

Shale Mtn.
7612

A

6500

To
Missoula,
37 mi

4500

5500

N

6000

Rhodes Peak
7930

G

6500

12

Granite
Pass

FOREST

E

Lolo
Pass

7000

Crooked

Fork

5500

Cayuse Creek

Proposed Great Burn Wilderness

6000

LOLO

5500

5500

0   8 km

0   5 mi

ELEVATIONS IN FEET
CONTOUR INTERVAL 500 FT

TRAIL

4500

5500

5000

12

6000

5000

To Kooskia,
83 mi

Lochsa

River

ground were St. Johnswort, pussytoes, yellow penstemons, and cinquefoils, all so small I had to bend low to appreciate their dainty beauty.

From the crest of the ridge we looked down upon a small, unnamed lake at the base of a glacier-scoured basin. We angled our way down, only to ascend another chute more formidable and rockier than the first. The flowers acquired an extraordinary fascination, especially since they provided me with a noble reason to stop and catch my breath.

Our roller coaster route took us through a graveyard of snags and across a talus slope stippled with yellow flowers that somehow found sustenance in the rubble of sharp-edged shale. We stopped beside a patch of snow and flavored cups of it with strawberry Kool-Aid for a hiker's treat known as slushies. Not long after, Dale declared lunchtime at 11 o'clock—none too soon for any of us, though we had already snacked twice along the way.

We had been traveling south in the direction of Rhodes Peak, at 7,930 feet the highest mountain in the Great Burn. Although there are more than 200 miles of trails, Dale generally avoids them, preferring to take off cross-country.

"Walking a trail, you tend to look down at your feet. But when you're bushwhacking, you need to keep track of where you've been and where you're going. You become more attentive, more intimate with the environment," Dale told me with a note of emphasis in his voice.

By midafternoon Rhodes Peak was still two steep ridges away, and so we abandoned our vague plan to climb it. Instead, we headed up 7,612-foot Shale Mountain, a gaunt, gray jumble of rock. The mountain looked imposing enough to give us a sense of accomplishment if we reached the summit. We did.

From the top we could see more than a hundred miles in all directions—a maze of mountains and valleys that included several national wildernesses—the Selway-Bitterroot, the Rattlesnake, the Bob Marshall, and Mission Mountains. Not a town or a paved road was visible.

The land was as untamed as it was in 1805, when Meriwether Lewis and William Clark followed what was later known as the Lolo Trail through Indian country. Their journal says they were "compelled to kill a Colt for our men & Selves to eat for the want of meat." The mountains, short of game, "much fatigued" the men and horses by "steep assents" in country "thickley covered with pine" and "much falling timber."

Today this Lewis and Clark country—just at the edge of the southern boundary of the proposed Great Burn wilderness—is still densely forested. To the north live numerous deer and elk, feeding on the abundant forage that sprouted in the burned acreage. A botanist might also detect a wider distribution of lodgepole pine, a species so adapted to the recurrent fires of the region that its cones, which are sealed by resin, can be opened by the heat of fire to release their seeds.

Some people say they have entered the wilderness when they're driving along a highway with a forest on both sides. Others need to be three days from a trailhead. For me, the five days I spent camped at Leo Lake was quintessential wilderness. We led a slow-paced, self-contained existence, enjoying our fellowship and finding satisfaction in the basic tasks of cooking, collecting firewood, and keeping warm and dry. I wish I could say I felt at home. What I did feel was an intense awareness of being an interloper in an alien and somewhat threatening realm.

But then take someone like silver-haired writer, forester, and trapper Bud Moore, who was raised in the Lolo Pass area and has lived in wild country for nearly all of his 70 years. "I see myself as a part of nature's intricate community and have learned how to fit in. I know how to interact with a grizzly far better than I can do a two-step," he told me the day after I returned from Leo Lake and visited him on his remote homestead, a private parcel in the Flathead National Forest. We talked in his spacious log cabin, whose wide windows frame scenes of deer, elk, bears, and hawks.

"I was 12 years old, on one of my first big trips alone in those mountains. One day I got into some dense brush, following a moose trail, and suddenly a big grizzly came around a boulder and walked toward me, with its nose low to the ground and head wagging from side to side. My first thought was I'd better make the first shot good. When I cocked the hammer of my .30-30 Winchester rifle, the bear heard the click. It stood up but never chomped its teeth, which is a sign of anger. Then it dropped down on all fours, and not a twig cracked as it disappeared.

"Now, I'd just speak softly to him. Black bears panic easily and run away, but the grizzly is a slow, deliberate animal. When confronted at close quarters, it's best to give him plenty of space, time, and friendly vibes. After all, we are old friends."

A lanky, vigorous man with a doctorate in science, Bud is quick to warn that behind the beauty of a wilderness like Great Burn lurks danger, unless you have the savvy and skills of good woodmanship. "You should be able to build a fire in wet, raw weather, to predict which way a bear will go from the nature of the terrain, and to assess avalanche risks in winter," he told me. "You should know enough to give yourself plenty of margin."

Years of experience have also made a modern-day mountain man of Don Aldrich, past president of the Montana Wildlife Federation. "People tell me I shouldn't be out there alone. But I reply, 'If something should happen, don't look for me. I'm where I want to be,'" he said. Until recent years, few but hunters, fishermen, and prospectors entered the Great Burn. Don is one of the hunters who have traditionally used the area to put an elk in the freezer for the winter.

"Elk does not taste as gamy as deer, and I hunt for the meat as well as for sport. It's also nice to have a big campfire with everybody sitting on a log, eating peanuts, drinking beer, and exaggerating the success of past big-game seasons," said Don, who, like Bud Moore, seems to have found the fountain of youth in Montana's rugged backcountry.

Don also goes after grouse, flushing them out of "hot spots"—the dwarf huckleberry patches, where they feed. "The young ones are good eating," he said. "Otherwise the birds are so tough you have trouble sticking a fork into the gravy."

Don doesn't like traveling by horse because a horse's demands limit the places the rider can camp. "With a horse you need a place with feed and water," Don said. "I've spent nights leaning against a tree to keep from rolling downhill. Level places are sometimes hard to find in the Burn."

I thought about that as I set out with Mike, Kathryn, and devout fly fisherman Don Snow on a two-day horseback trip to the Siamese Lakes, some 11 miles up the Straight Creek Trail. We started out at the Hole in the Wall Lodge, just outside the proposed wilderness boundary, where wranglers Steve Thompson and his wife, Cheri, along with Greg Newman, were loading mules with gear. "Mantying," they called it, probably from the Spanish word for the coarse cloth used to wrap loads.

"The main thing in loading is balance," said Steve, cinching the various bundles with knots designed for quick release, in case an animal stumbles in the brush. "A mule can carry as much as 100 pounds on each side, but I try to keep it down to 75.

"For packing there's no comparison between a mule and a horse; a mule will carry a heavier load, easier, and farther on less food, and it is more surefooted. A mule will step off a trail or go around a tree to avoid knocking a pack off, while a horse will bump and bang the panniers all over the place."

Steve signaled it was time to head out, and Don Snow gingerly heaved himself up on Wally's back, remarking that the horse got him too far off the ground. Don is a master of the sport and art of fly-fishing, which he describes as chasing trout with little bits of feather or tufts of fur or animal hair.

Anglers have a special way of looking at a river, reading the water like a topographical map. I discovered this as we rode along, following the trail upstream. Most of the way, Don kept his eyes on Straight Creek, taking note of the pools, eddies, and riffles, and assessing the spillways where boulders shattered the water, transforming quiet runs into rapids.

"The way a river bends and deepens tells me a lot about where the fish hang out," Don said, beating his way through some brush with his fishing-rod case. We were traveling through one of the Great Burn's lush, timbered draws that had escaped the fires at the beginning of the century. A variety of berry bushes also flanked the trail.

"If I were on foot, I could eat my way up here," Don said wistfully, as we progressed uphill. After about three hours we dismounted beside a series of small waterfalls. While we waited for Cheri and the pack train she was leading, Don wasted no time. He sloshed along the riverbank, stalking the stream for rising trout. Mike focused on a cluster of white cabbage butterflies that hovered around some flat black boulders.

"I wonder what all the butterflies are doing around here?" Mike asked.

"They're probably asking the same thing about us," Cheri replied.

For a while, I basked in the mellow sweetness of the day and watched a red-tailed hawk slowly trace invisible circles in the cloudless sky.

"I'll bet it just flapped its wings a few times and has been riding the thermals all morning," Cheri observed. She lingered only for a time, and then the pack train plodded on ahead.

Rising from the lowlands, where evergreens locked the land in year-round shade, were the open slopes so characteristic of the Great Burn. On one, fire had mowed down a forest, and the snags littered the ground like pickup sticks after a wild toss.

When we remounted, I caught up with Don, who assured me that the best time to cast a fly was yet to come: "When it's so dark you can hardly see the water."

Ahead of us lay the difficult, almost vertical climb up Chilkoot Pass. Difficult, that is, for the heaving horses, shiny with sweat. More arduous and unnerving for me was the descent on the other side. The horses threaded their way down a slope so precipitous that when I looked at my stirrups I saw the ground falling away beneath me.

But nothing, not even my trepidation, could diminish the vibrant beauty of that meadow ablaze with a galaxy of flowers. Like an Impressionist painting, the meadow shimmered with a blur of color—no dominant hues but a heady collage of red, yellow, pink, white, purple, and even the black of the odd, olive-shaped coneflower, all displayed against a background of resonant green.

In high spirits we arrived at the lower Siamese Lake, where we pitched tents for the night, and I came to know something of the lore and wizardry of fly-fishing.

"Some people needlessly complicate matters. Basically, it's hitting it right, being there when the fish are," said Don as he scanned the shore. The lake's smooth water was dimpled by trout rising to the surface to feed on insects. "When there's a sudden hatch and the trout go on a feeding binge, then anyone can reel them in. When no hatch is on, you have to use flies that imitate insects or small fish. Usually you match the insects in size, color, and general form." Don opened a small box that contained about 200 hand-tied flies.

"Occasionally, I'll fish with an attractor, a fly that triggers a trout's curiosity. Either way the goal is to have the fly hit the water first, so it just drops naturally, like a bug," he said, demonstrating a technique that whipped 40 yards of line effortlessly across the water. "As soon as a fish feels the steel of a hook, it's in a hurry to get away. So you have to set the hook real fast. Sometimes I think the real reason we are able to catch anything is because the fish finally take pity on us."

How else, of course, could I have landed one!

My journey to the Great Burn ended with a trip in the northern section of the proposed wilderness. Part of the ride was along a stretch of the ridge-top State Line Trail, a rough but spectacular route whose sweeping vistas were embellished by sparkling lakes. At the invitation of Orville Daniels, supervisor of the Lolo National Forest, Mike and I joined an official trip to survey conditions on the Montana side of the wilderness. We rode for three days. At times I wished I had saddled what Orville calls the perfect horse, "which walks as well as a Tennessee walker, rides as easy as a mule, has the durability of a quarter horse, and is as smart as a donkey."

Parts of the days were devoted to pondering ways to protect the land and regulate its future use. The questions came down to this: How do we manage enough to protect ecosystems without managing too much? No easy answers were forthcoming. But the Forest Service officials agreed that wilderness is a resource as vital as timber and water. And, fortunate enough to experience the Great Burn, we all knew that its natural splendor is something to cherish and to preserve.

In a blur of cascading beauty, the West Fork of Fish Creek purls through a colonnade of towering red cedars (opposite). On the lush bank, dense with old timber that escaped the full fury of devastating fire, raindrops spangle an emerald tapestry of oak ferns (below). A toxic fly agaric mushroom, with its characteristic white patches, emerges (upper) from a bed of pine needles along Cache Creek.

FOLLOWING PAGES: Swollen with snowmelt, Straight Creek spills down a natural stairway. Alongside, a trail cuts through brush where summer berries abound.

"The sport
and art
of...chasing trout
with little
bits
of feather."

Sharp-edged ridge, honed by ice in ages past, rims a nameless Montana lake (opposite). Fewer than 50 visitors a year enter this glacial basin, a favorite retreat of conservationist Dale Harris. In the sudden winter of a July squall, Dale, with rod, and Kathryn Evers, (below) set out on a fishing expedition. Two cutthroat trout (above) did not get away. Named for the red slash below the jaw, this combative species often leaps for flies, striking more actively in evening.

"Our
roller coaster
route
took us
through
a graveyard
of snags."

Solitary mountain goat stands sentinel in Clearwater National Forest (opposite).
About 30 of the nimble climbers roam the high country here, in a land that still
bears snags (above) and scars left by the "Big Blowup" of 1910.

FOLLOWING PAGES: *Like a fallen cloud, morning mist drifts past open slopes near*
Leo Lake. By creating open spaces that fostered the growth of forage—grasses,
shrubs, and shoots—forest fires have increased the area's wildlife population.

105

Summer brings the benediction of flowers to a Chilkoot Pass meadow (opposite).
Scarlet Indian paintbrush (below right), white yarrow, and purple daisies
dominate the crest. On the trail to French Lake, horsemint blossoms (below)
cluster atop a square stem, an identifying trait of this aromatic family.

"The vibrant
beauty
of that meadow
ablaze
with a galaxy
of flowers."

As daylight departs, subalpine firs cast long shadows on lower Siamese Lake (opposite). "The open bowls with timbered draws are places where elk like to hang out," says wrangler Steve Thompson, who rides with Kathryn Evers down to the lake from Chilkoot Pass (below). Once an Indian hunting ground, the Great Burn now gets hunters who ride in, hoping to bring down an elk.

FOLLOWING PAGES: On tall stalks, blossoms of beargrass spike a meadow scarcely touched by a human hand. Those who come from the outside world walk lightly here, awed before the subtle beauty of an enclave shaped by fire and ice.

Arctic Awakening
With Brief Spring Comes Renewal

Summer's splurge of light reveals harsh contours in Alaska's eastern Brooks Range. To the north lies the tundra with its annual explosion of life.

They appeared suddenly, a broad stream of gray pouring over a low ridge along the bank of the Kongakut River in northeastern Alaska. In the thousands they passed, grunting so loud they drowned out the sounds of the river. For 40 minutes they surged by, less than 200 feet away, their legs producing a strange clicking. It was 2 a.m., and the sun rested low in the northern sky. The valley lay in deep shadow cast by the high peaks of the Brooks Range.

The caribou before me were some of the 45,000 that had left the Porcupine herd on the coastal plain near the Arctic Ocean and moved south. Some massed on a hillside above the river. Others congregated on vast fields of ice in the valley. Still others, a seething torrent of bulls, cows, and calves, kept flowing into the valley. The leg clicking I kept hearing may have been caused by the snap of tendons or moving bones.

Standing in the shadows watching the caribou, I recalled my first impression of Alaska's northernmost mountain range some 20 years earlier during a winter flight to Barrow on the Arctic Ocean. I had looked down through the blue-gray dusk of high noon at an endless jumble of frozen valleys and snowy windswept summits, and I had thought it looked like a barren and inhospitable land, a desolate corner of some uninhabitable planet.

Now I had returned to the north to explore a vast wilderness area that stretched from the edge of the boreal forest north across the Brooks Range and coastal plain to the Arctic Ocean and eastward into Canada's Yukon Territory. During a summer of hiking, rafting, canoeing, camping, and flying I was discovering just how wrong my first impression had been.

Most of the area was within the Arctic National Wildlife Refuge, a 19.2-million-acre tract set aside to preserve an enormous but delicate ecosystem. All of the area lies well north of the Arctic Circle, and about 8 million acres are designated as wilderness. I also visited Canada's Northern Yukon National Park, which adjoins the refuge.

It was springtime when I returned to the Arctic, but for weeks a heavy pall of clouds and fog, spawned by the massive ice pack of the Arctic Ocean, had hung over the coastal plain. Snow refused to melt in the caribou's calving ground, and most of the animals lingered east of the Alaskan border in Canada's Yukon Territory.

I took off from Fairbanks with pilot Don Ross and flew northeast, determined to find the calving caribou. Gradually, as we headed northward, the deep summery green of Fairbanks paled and then vanished.

We finally found the caribou—thousands of cows, many already with calves—spread out over a broad area near the Spring River in the Yukon Territory, several miles south of the coast. Don landed on a frozen lake, plowing through a couple of snowdrifts before we came to a stop. I stepped out and put on a heavy wool shirt and a parka. Summer suddenly seemed a long way off.

On a small rise at the edge of the lake we set up camp, made hot tea, and cooked dinner. It was already past midnight. The sun lay just above the horizon in the north. Caribou grazed on the tundra or moved slowly across the far edge of the lake, toward the northwest.

Sleep did not come quickly. My initial sensation of silence soon gave way to a realization that sounds of life were everywhere. All around us birds were proclaiming their territories and going through elaborate courtship rituals. And when the caribou came close, their grunts filled the air.

Several times I was awakened by raucous calls of ptarmigan just outside the tent. The long cackle usually ended with a loud cry that sounded like someone coarsely yelling *Go back! Go back! Go back!* There was no real night. The sun sank lower in the sky around midnight, only to rise high again as it circled toward the south.

When I emerged from the tent in the morning, male Lapland long-spurs soared 40 or 50 feet overhead in crystal air, hovered a moment, and then fluttered down with a beautiful, clear melodious trill. Again and again the ritual was repeated as the males sought to woo the females.

On slow, rhythmic wings an arctic tern flew toward the coast, scanning the frozen lake for signs of food. Of all the birds that come from afar to summer along this frigid coast, the arctic tern journeys the farthest, from the Antarctic all the way to here, at the other end of the earth.

Don and I crossed a small hill to reach the Spring River, skirting boggy channels of meltwater. Because the ground is sealed by permafrost less than a finger's length below the surface, water from melting snow has no place to go. It collects in an endless maze of bogs, ponds, and lakes, a perfect breeding ground for the billions of mosquitoes that emerge during the short arctic summer. Coarse tussocks of grass crowd the bogs, making walking a tiring ordeal.

I sat near the river and listened to the steady lap of water against an undercut bank of ice and the dry rustle of wind in last year's dead grass. A few hundred scattered caribou, mostly cows with calves, grazed on a hillside nearby. A few calves stayed with their mothers and nursed. Others frolicked, racing away from their mothers only to turn and run back again, wind rippling their soft, light brown hair.

Suddenly another group came running over the hill, spooking the nearby animals. They all ran off together. In a moment a familiar shape ambled over the crest of the hill, and I knew what had startled the caribou.

"Here, have a look," I said, handing the binoculars to Don.

"A fur ball," he said. "With teeth."

Three species of bears inhabit this northern wilderness. Black bears are found only south of the Brooks Range. North of the mountains are grizzlies and polar bears, though grizzlies also range widely south of the mountains. This was a grizzly. We watched him lumber downhill toward us. He stopped and sniffed to left and right, then continued in our direction. He had blood on his fur.

We were getting a bit nervous, so we backed down out of sight and started circling to our left. The bear began running at full speed. He cut across the tundra, lunging headlong through puddles and over bogs, spray glittering in the sun like showers of diamonds as he ran.

He crossed out of sight over the last ridge, about three miles away. He was still running. He had caught our scent and obviously didn't want anything to do with us. That attitude suited Don and me just fine.

Later, on the hilltop where the grizzly had appeared, we came across a newborn caribou. It got up on wobbly legs and walked a few steps, then stumbled, and fell down again. I approached to take pictures. The calf watched me through deep brown eyes, a bit nervously at first. It dozed for a moment, awoke, and stood up. It sniffed at my face from only a few inches away, stumbled over to my camera tripod, and sniffed again, looking, I think, for a place to nurse. Finally it flopped down on the tundra.

Don and I saw the calf's mother circling at the base of the hill, so we backed away and waited. The mother continued circling until she caught the calf's scent. Then she turned and made a beeline to the spot. She nudged the calf, and slowly they moved off. Her newborn seemed to gain strength with every step.

The caribou are international citizens, wandering freely back and forth between Canada and the United States, following migratory routes impressed in their collective instinct over millennia. They know no national boundaries. At first it seemed they were everywhere. A few days later they were gone, headed west toward Alaska.

After Don dropped me off at the Kongakut and headed back to the south, I began to lose track of the days, often wandering along rivers, past valleys, and over ridges in the middle of the night, when the low midnight

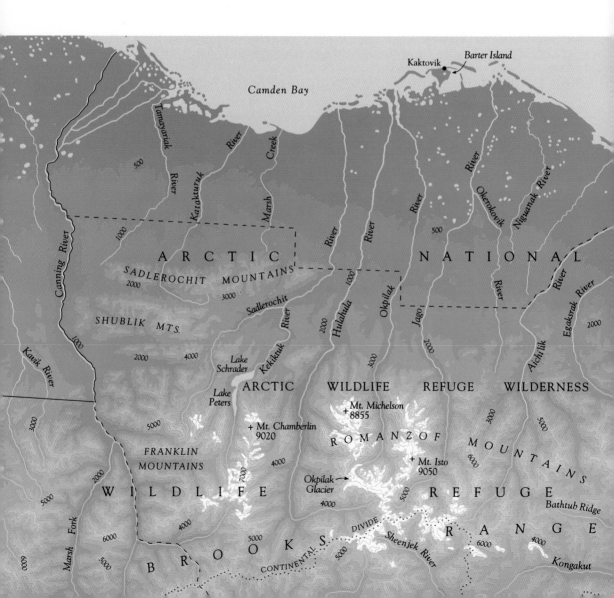

sun painted the landscape with rich contrasts of light and shadow. Summer came to the north tentatively at first, cautiously nudging back the edge of winter. Then the endless days arrived, their warmth bursting over the Arctic in an explosion of new life.

Waterfowl flew northward, following behind the melting edge of ice and snow. Sometimes I saw them coming in too early, geese or ducks skidding to a comic crash-landing on the surface of a lake not yet thawed. Sandpipers, swans, plovers, and terns arrived to court and mate and build their nests in the wake of the vanishing snow.

The green of summer comes to the south side of the mountains first,

An ecosystem born in the Ice Age awaited the author in a roadless wilderness of mountain and tundra above the Arctic Circle. Within the Arctic National Wildlife Refuge in Alaska and the adjoining Northern Yukon National Park in Canada dwell caribou, wolves, bears, and musk-oxen. Unlike wildlife, people crossing the U.S.-Canadian border must find an authorized entry.

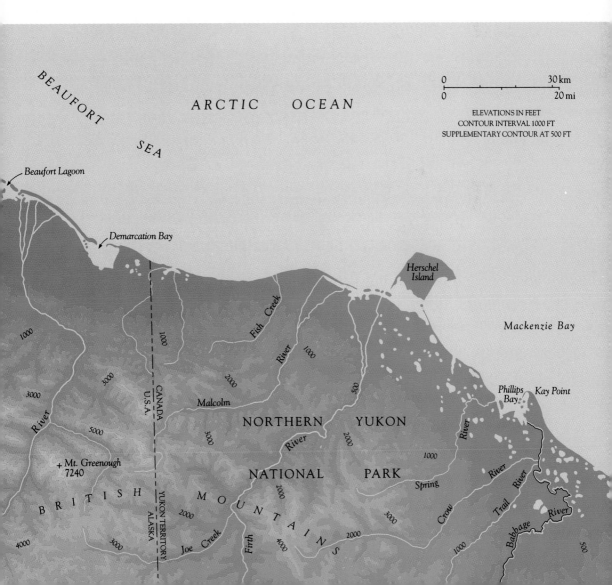

ELEVATIONS IN FEET
CONTOUR INTERVAL 1000 FT
SUPPLEMENTARY CONTOUR AT 500 FT

0   30 km
0   20 mi

BEAUFORT

SEA

ARCTIC   OCEAN

Beaufort Lagoon

Demarcation Bay

Herschel Island

Mackenzie Bay

Fish Creek

River

1000

1000

2000

500

Malcolm

Phillips Bay

Kay Point

NORTHERN   YUKON

River

2000

River

3000

CANADA
U.S.A.

3000

3000

1000

+ Mt. Greenough
7240

NATIONAL   PARK

Spring

River

River

5000

River

1000

B   R   I   T   I   S   H

M   O   U   N   T   A   I   N   S

2000

YUKON TERRITORY
ALASKA

Crow

Trail River

River

Babbage

River

4000

3000

2000

Joe Creek

Firth

4000

2000

3000

1000

500

spreading over patches of willows, poplars, and cottonwoods that mingle with spruce. The green climbs the valleys quickly, leapfrogs over the mountains, and spills down northern valleys toward the coastal plain. The coast, chilled by the massive ice pack of the Arctic Ocean, is the last to turn green.

Purple mountain saxifrages, arctic forget-me-nots, woolly louseworts, and northern primroses pop out at the very edge of retreating snow. In sheltered spots, even north of the mountains, microclimates allow small stands of cottonwoods and poplars to survive. But over most of the north, plants cling to the spongy tundra soil that is sandwiched between devastating arctic winds and permanently frozen ground only inches below. There, even the robust willow may grow only an inch or two high.

Summer was well on its way by mid-June, when I joined a group of visitors for a raft trip down the Hulahula River, whose name was bestowed many years ago by whalers from Hawaii. The Hulahula rises among glaciers of the Brooks Range's highest peaks and follows a deep glacial valley north toward the sea. The trip had been proposed by Susan Alexander of the Wilderness Society and organized by our guide, Jim Campbell of Fairbanks. My wife, Marilyn, had flown north to join me. Eleven of us traveled in three rafts.

We arrived on a spectacular evening. The sun glistened on freshly snowcapped crests that towered over deep, moody valleys. Cloud shadows, dark and sober, danced across peaks glazed with patches of sunshine. Beyond the river, dozens of Dall's sheep grazed in high, craggy hollows. Even at a distance we could see the magnificent curved horns of the rams.

In late morning we loaded the rafts and pushed out into the current. Marilyn and I shared a raft with Ginny Wood, a woman long experienced in the ways of Alaskan wilderness. Our boatman was Randy Udall, a superbly fit young outdoorsman from Colorado. His positive attitude and indefatigable good humor brightened our trip even on the stormiest of days.

As we set out, black curtains of rain shrouded the mountain peaks. Squalls moved in and broadened into a full-scale storm. We struggled to paddle into a swift head wind. Then the wind shifted 180 degrees, and we raced down the valley.

"Forward! Forward!" Randy commanded as he guided us along the deeper channels. "Hold! Backpaddle!"

We occasionally came aground with a crunch where the river spread out over a wide gravel bar and became too shallow for our raft. Then we would all climb out and push the raft to deeper water.

We stopped to make camp at a spot incredibly beautiful in spite of the rain. Beyond a big rock jutting into the river a tiny clear stream joined the silty water of the Hulahula. Rosy blossoms of dwarf rhododendron brightened a hillside overlooking the camp. Next morning, when sunshine on the tent awakened me at 3:30 a.m., raindrops still sparkled on the rhododendrons and hung heavily from delicate white blossoms of bell heather.

Sunday, June 21st, was a long day—the longest of the year. We set out through vast sheets of *aufeis*, ice formed when flowing water freezes upon the surface of an already frozen river. Some of the sheets had not melted completely. Paddling along a meandering channel cut into the aufeis, we were startled by the occasional boom of ice crashing into the river.

We shot several of our best rapids that day, pausing to survey them first, then bursting through the waves with cheers and shouts. We bailed as we floated along between rapids. Finally, where the Hulahula broke out of the mountains and began a more gentle drop over the coastal plain, we pulled ashore.

"Hey! There's a bear," someone shouted. We watched as it passed near our campsite and disappeared into a willow thicket. Before we had finished pitching our tents, someone else spied another grizzly upriver. We watched that one until, like the first, it vanished into the brush.

About then, Marilyn, busy unpacking gear in our tent, looked out— and saw a bushy creature approaching only a few feet away. With grizzlies on the mind, her first reaction was, "It's a cub!" For a moment she expected to see its angry mother close behind. But this fur ball turned out to be merely a porcupine. Displeased with the attention it attracted, it quickly waddled away. We finished dinner late, and at midnight we all raised our cups to toast the summer solstice. But with summer having only barely arrived, the sun would descend farther each day until night and winter returned to the north.

After a day of hiking we returned to the river, which became increasingly braided as it flowed through the coastal plain. Often we had to drag our raft off gravel bars. We battled a stiff crosswind trying to keep away from the bank. During a break ashore we saw bunches of wool, softer than cashmere, hanging in riverside bushes. This was qiviut, the wool of the musk-ox. Later we spotted a herd of the marvelous shaggy beasts, which looked like creatures out of the Pleistocene. One patriarch of the herd of 14 had such a long coat that it dragged the ground around his hooves. The musk-oxen approached until, spooked by our presence, they ran.

Hunters killed off Alaska's musk-oxen in the 19th century. In the 1930s musk-oxen from Greenland were brought in to reintroduce the species to Alaska. In 1969 and 1970 some of their descendants were placed on the tundra of the coastal plain. They now number nearly 600.

A few days after the raft trip ended, I was on my way north again with Don Ross. July 1 was drawing near, and vast numbers of caribou could appear on the coastal plain at any time. Ken Whitten, a biologist from the Alaska Department of Fish and Game, was coordinating a caribou census that combined counts in both the Arctic National Wildlife Refuge and Northern Yukon National Park. Flying with pilot Dennis Miller, Ken kept track of herd movements by monitoring signals from radio collars around the necks of 72 caribou.

One evening Ken and Dennis landed near the camp Don and I had set up at the Aichilik River. We soon began talking about caribou. I asked Ken what drove the animals to mass on the plains at this time of year.

"There are two theories," he said. "One is insect avoidance. The other is social. I tend to agree with the first. The more they group together, the less each individual is bothered by mosquitoes." I agreed. There's a big difference between a lot of mosquitoes on one caribou and the same number of mosquitoes on tens of thousands of caribou.

The summer aggregation, whatever its inspiration, afforded a chance to take aerial photographs so the caribou could be counted. "I wouldn't be surprised if we count 200,000 this year," Ken said. (They counted 165,000.)

After the journey to the Kongakut's valley to see the great massing of caribou there, Don and I flew to the coastal plain. We landed on a patch of tundra beside the Sadlerochit River and set up camp about a mile from the shore of Camden Bay. One day, walking west along the coast, we found an Eskimo whaling lookout made of driftwood. For centuries the Arctic Ocean has provided a wealth of marine mammals—whales, polar bears, seals, and walrus—vital to the Eskimo's survival.

Now everything was quiet except for the constant rush of wind and the splash of waves on the beach. Beyond a stretch of open water the ice glistened. A pair of swans, slow and graceful, lifted from a pond and turned to soar with the wind. An eider rose from a cove where stocky sea ducks—old-squaws—paddled on the waves. To the south, beyond the coastal plain, the mountains rose in long blue ridges, peaks crested with snow and glacial ice.

I was moved by the immense expanse of coastal plain, ice always drifting offshore, the constant wind. For the only time during the entire summer I felt the vast loneliness of the place.

Everywhere, camouflaged among clumps of sedges or dwarf willows, we found nests of birds—longspurs, jaegers, ptarmigan, white-crowned sparrows, golden plovers. A sandpiper nest near camp had four eggs. It was filled with lively speckled chicks when we left four days later.

We flew east along the coast to observe vast congregations of caribou, tens of thousands massed together. They bunched up on sheets of aufeis, waded into the sea, or moved slowly in gray-brown waves across the tundra. I thought of herds of wildebeest I had seen in Africa and understood why this area is sometimes called the Serengeti of the north.

When the caribou census ended, I joined Glenn Elison, the refuge manager, and Michael Rees, also from the U.S. Fish and Wildlife Service, on a survey trip to the Okpilak valley. The valley, because of its glacial features and scenic beauty, has been recommended for natural landmark status by the National Park Service.

We arrived in a pouring rain at the confluence of two streams walled in by rust-stained gray-and-black cliffs on one side and a saw-toothed ridge on the other. The rivers churned with runoff from rain and melting glaciers, boulders clunking along the riverbed.

The valley was a charmed place. The rain tapered off by the time we set up camp. Yellow cinquefoil and fuchsia fireweed brightened fields green with arctic willows, mosses, sedges, lichens, and grass. Upriver, cotton grass danced in the wind. A grizzly foraged across the water. Downriver, another stream shot out of a side canyon and plunged over a 30-foot waterfall. Nourished by mist, a miniature forest of lichens grew nearby.

About four miles above camp, we came to walls of moraine, broken rock debris chewed out of the mountains by glacial action. Rain fell as we crossed the moraine. When the rain stopped, a mist rose from jumbled mounds of rock, creating a surrealistic landscape.

Beyond a final ridge, we looked out over a lake to the glittering mass of the Okpilak Glacier, its tongue of ice laced with streamlets of meltwater. We circled the lake and climbed high enough on the glacier to see the mountainous source of the ice—crevassed snowfields hanging from frosty peaks. Windswept clouds blackened the steep ridges that hemmed in a glistening cascade of ice.

"Everything here in the refuge is so spectacular," Michael said later, "that the word begins to lose its impact from being repeated so often."

"This refuge," Glenn pointed out, "is larger than all the other refuges in all the other 49 states put together. And, except for the Aleutians, it's the most remote."

The remoteness limits access. Vast areas remain virtually untouched; most recreational visitors go to areas accessible by aircraft. Some of this may change. Even as I explored this pristine wilderness, in Washington Congress was debating proposals to open the coastal plain for petroleum exploration. Oil companies see in the area the potential for another Prudhoe Bay oil field bonanza. Conservationists fear the loss of a wilderness as well as the disruption of a major caribou calving area and destruction of nesting sites for a multitude of migratory birds.

Keith Crowder of the University of Alaska, a geologist who has spent years unraveling mysteries locked in the stone of the Brooks Range, spoke about the petroleum exploration. "We do need the oil, and there's probably lots of it there," he said, confessing a troubled ambivalence about seeing the region developed. "Mankind needs wilderness, too, places where he knows he can go and be alone with nature that's undisturbed. That also has value. And there's not much real wilderness left in the world."

To spend a week alone with the wilderness, I flew to Schrader and Peters lakes. On a hill overlooking Lake Schrader, I set up my tent as sporadic rainbows appeared and faded above whitecaps whipped by the wind.

All next day the wind blew, but toward evening I found a tiny quiet cove and cast my lure into the water. On the first cast I pulled ashore a fighting arctic char. I looked it over, measured it, and returned it to the water. At 26 inches, it was far more than I could eat.

My second cast brought in a 20-inch char. Fried with salt and lemon-pepper and accompanied by boiled potatoes and sautéed onions, it was delicious. Half of it I saved for breakfast the next day.

The wind quit as I ate dinner, and I sat on the shore watching fog silently drift in over the hills and settle on the lake. A plaintive cry broke the stillness. An arctic loon had surfaced just offshore, a gray ghost riding on silver-rippled water. Several times he called, slowly paddling out toward the fog; and from somewhere far in the mist came the equally forlorn reply of his mate.

An hour later the water was like gray glass fading into a fog that obliterated everything from view but the shore at my feet. It was well past midnight and silence blanketed everything.

I had brought a collapsible canoe. I readied it, eased it into the water, and for an hour I glided through a silent world of fog.

Later I loaded my canoe and paddled across Schrader and through the narrow entry to Lake Peters, continuing for about four and a half more miles to the end of the lake, where I set up camp. For a week I canoed, fished, and hiked. Once I sat motionless in pounding rain for two and a half hours while 15 bull caribou wandered into my camp, grazing. They lay down, some within 50 feet of me, before eventually moving away.

After a week at the lakes, I flew south to end my trip with Joe Want, a professional hunting guide, at his camp in the upper Sheenjek River valley. Joe normally uses two horses and four mules to carry his gear into the Sheenjek, a good two-week journey from the road to Prudhoe Bay. I had planned to walk with him part way, but this year high water made the trip impossible. Joe had to fly in to his camp.

Joe, a guide since 1964, has come to the Sheenjek every year since 1972, bringing in hunters. He's a wiry man, strong in body and strong in opinion. And of wildlife and wilderness he speaks lyrically.

"Most of all I like the solitude," he says, "especially when I come in with the animals in July and take them out again in September. I'm usually alone then; I rarely see another person on the way out.

"There's fresh snow, and I know everything that is happening by the tracks. It is so phenomenally clear. At night the sky is like one big star. When there's a full moon, visibility is as good as in the day. Yet there's an eeriness, an awesomeness you never experience by day."

On my last day at camp I awoke at 2 a.m. Fog filled the valley. A deep dusk blended with the fog to mute the colors of the landscape and silhouette the dead willows that stood around our camp. There was a chill in the air, and the scent that sometimes comes with the changing of the seasons.

Already in mid-August I had noted the signs of fall: a patch of bearberries and lingonberries turned scarlet, a sprig of willow turning yellow, a few golden leaves on the scrub birch. They were harbingers of the time to come, when the land would blaze with colors beyond imagination.

I walked beyond the willows onto the gravel and listened to the whisper of the river over rock, but I could not see the river in the fog. A wolf passed that night. In the morning I found its tracks. It had approached from downriver, scented the camp, and turned away, moving unseen.

I thought of the months ahead. Frost would come to decorate the autumn leaves, and ice would still the voice of the river. The grizzly would find his den. Moose would move to the valleys and into the willow thickets. Wolves would follow.

The sun would drop lower and lower into the southern sky, appearing more and more briefly each day until it slid permanently below the horizon, and only the stars and moon would remain to bathe the frozen land in eerie light. From time to time the aurora borealis would flare overhead, and its curtains of light would dance across the sky.

Under a gradually thickening blanket of white, once again the land would sleep.

North of the tree line and deep in the Brooks Range, 6,000-foot Bathtub Ridge shows its ribs, marine shales. Runoff from snowmelt and rain have grooved the steep slope. The shales endure as relics of the region's oceanic past.

Borne on the tides of migration, members of the Porcupine caribou herd wade the icy waters of the Kongakut. Each spring the 165,000-strong herd moves 400 miles through the mountains to its calving grounds on the tundra. The herd gets its name from the Porcupine River, which runs through the caribou winter range in the Yukon. A Canadian-born calf only hours old (right) beholds the author for what is most likely the only time in its life that it will see a human being.

FOLLOWING PAGES: Field of plenty, the spacious tundra at Beaufort Lagoon attracts a sprawl of caribou that pause to feed on grasses, moss, and lichens. Breezes from the nearby Arctic Ocean keep mosquito hordes at bay.

DONALD E. ROSS

127

Converging from points around the world, millions of migrating birds collect on the tundra in summer to mate and nest. The coastal plain attracts about 100 bird species during the Arctic's short summer. An arctic tern (opposite, upper) flew in from the Antarctic, some 12,000 miles away, on the longest migratory trip in the animal world. Camouflaged on the spongy ground, a lesser golden plover (below) arrived from the Southern Hemisphere. A willow ptarmigan (opposite, lower) guards his territory. By winter he and his kind will have molted and turned snow-white. A year-round resident of Alaska, the willow ptarmigan is the state bird.

"I was awakened
    by raucous calls
 of ptarmigan
       just outside
    the tent."

"The low midnight sun painted the landscape."

In the dead of a summer night, sunlight streams over the upper Sheenjek River valley in the Arctic National Wildlife Refuge. Light banishes darkness north of the Arctic Circle during June and most of July. With the tilt of the North Pole sunward, the sky stays lit for 24 hours a day. Mirroring the hue of the midnight sun, a pasqueflower (opposite) glories in its brief season of life.

Alone on nature's stage, the author, in a self-timed photograph, paddles on Lake Schrader. "With me there were only the birds and the wind," he says.

FOLLOWING PAGES: *Hikers tarry in a patch of cotton grass in glacier-carved Okpilak valley. Snow on the ridge recalls a long dark winter past.*

By Suzanne Venino

Photographs by Craig Aurness and Jonathan S. Blair

138

Desert Splendor
Mojave's Singing Dunes and Magic Mountains

Dark skies glower over the mountains and brush-studded flats of California's eastern Mojave Desert, a wind-whipped land of wild and brutal beauty.

The landscape is lean. At first it looks lifeless, a scorched earth where little grows. And what does grow is armed for a battle of survival in a land of little rain. But there is also beauty here. I found it in the fiery radiance of a cactus flower. I found it in the play of light on the mountains, when the midday sun softens into the pale pinks and gentle blues of sunset, magically cloaking mountains in ever-deepening shades of purple. I found it in the freedom of far horizons, in the timelessness of the land.

This place of stark beauty is the East Mojave National Scenic Area in southeastern California. From there the Mojave sprawls across southern Nevada into western Arizona and southern Utah. Most people speed through the desert, clocking their time in hours. But to know the desert takes patience, for it speaks quietly, with a subtle eloquence, and only those who take the time to listen will understand the beauty of this raw, unwatered land.

The Mojave is a desert of magnificent diversity. Mountain ranges dominate the landscape. Ancient lake beds shimmer with mind-bending illusions of water. Migrating waterfowl feed at lush oases. Rivers disappear underground. And sand dunes sing—basso profundo.

At Kelso Dunes the sands reward the long climb by playing a joyous tune. But conditions—such as dry sand, no humidity—must be just right. One day I climbed toward the dunes' sharp peaks, at 700 feet the third highest dune system in the United States. Formed over millennia as westerly winds bore sand from the Mojave River floodplain, Kelso Dunes looks like a great sleeping giant, forever restless as the winds shape and reshape its hulking form. White primrose crept along the foredunes, and slender stalks of ricegrass danced in the wind, tracing circles in the sand.

Halfway to the top, I stopped to rest near a desert willow. The tree appeared dead, a withered victim, it seemed, of desiccating winds, desert heat, and lack of water. Within moments the spring breezes that had accompanied me raged into fierce gusts, and the stinging sands made continuing unbearable. I turned and started down, to return on another, calmer day.

The sky was clear and the sun climbing high when I returned to Kelso Dunes. Again I stopped by the willow. Tiny green leaves now filigreed the drooping branches, and the tree was abloom with orchidlike flowers of the palest purple. Some desert plants, I would later learn, commonly adapt to dry spells by going dormant, dropping all leaves, and generally closing up shop. With life-giving rain, they burst into bloom.

After an hour of hiking I reached the top. With giant steps I bounded down the steep slope of the pyramid-shaped peak. Sand flowed around me. Then I heard it—low, resonant, like the notes of an organ. The harmonious chords were produced by smooth grains of quartz and feldspar rubbing against each other as they slid down the dry slip face of Kelso Dunes.

Except for scattered parcels of private land, the Bureau of Land Management administers 4.5 million acres of the eastern Mojave in California, protecting natural and cultural resources and overseeing such uses as grazing and mining. Nearly 15 million people live within a few hours' drive of the Mojave, and many are discovering it is not a wasteland but a playland, a place to camp, hike, jeep, backpack, bird-watch, rock climb, or photograph. In 1980, the Department of the Interior designated 1.5 million acres of public lands in the desert as the East Mojave National Scenic Area.

Travel can be rugged, and a four-wheel-drive vehicle is the preferred means for covering great distances. Indian trails, old wagon roads, mining roads, and powerline or waterline roads lead you to secluded places where the only sounds are the descending notes of the canyon wren and the rustle of lizards scurrying through the scrub.

I was led to Devils Playground because the name intrigued me and I wanted to see what was there. I had my choice of two routes from the town of Kelso, population 75. One was via a paved road that looped around to the north; the other was a faint set of jeep tracks that made a beeline across creosote-tufted plains. I decided that the tracks were a shortcut by a good five miles.

The primitive road was studded with sharp volcanic rocks. Scraggly, stunted vegetation poked from what looked like fire-blasted land. I slowed to a bouncing five miles per hour. An antelope ground squirrel, waving a white flag of a tail, raced alongside, easily outdistancing me.

I lost the way several times and had to backtrack. Stay calm, I mumbled to myself, mentally summarizing my situation. I had plenty of water but very little food. Before leaving, I had told friends where I was going, but they would not know my route. If I did not return, they would alert authorities and a search party would be dispatched. It's a big desert, though, and it could be days before anyone found me. I kept driving.

The tracks nearly disappeared as they snaked through a labyrinth of dry washes. I could not take the chance of stopping or even slowing down in the soft sand. So I kept up my speed, skidding and sliding as I made split-second decisions about which way to turn.

Two hours and 13 bone-jarring, nerve-wracking miles later, I came to an intersection. To the left another dirt track would take me to the Devils Playground; a turn to the right would lead back to civilization. I decided that Devils Playground could wait until another day.

The desert is a constant teacher, and I had learned a valuable lesson: a healthy respect for desert travel. Of the many dangers in the desert, getting lost is perhaps the most common. Getting lost without water, however, can be fatal, and I had been cautioned to carry more water than I thought I needed. Hildegard Gulley and her husband, Sarge, prospect for gold in the New York Mountains. They must haul 50 gallons of water from town every other day during the summer. "If I'm out of food, it don't worry me," Hildegard told me. "If I'm out of cigarettes, I get mean. But if I run out of water, I get scared."

The Mojave, on average, receives less than eight inches of rain a year. Yet water is a powerful force in shaping the desert's land and life. Violent summer storms here send flash floods roaring down the mountains, leaving in their wake gullies and washes that pattern the earth like veins on a leaf. The storms, once spent, soak quickly into parched soil. Winter snowmelt and drizzling rains give a more uniform watering. The only accurate description of desert rain, however, is that it's unpredictable.

Perennial shrubs soak up erratic rains with shallow, wide-spreading roots. Succulents, such as cactuses, store water for future use in expandable cell tissues. Seeds may lie dormant for years until sufficient rain falls, at just the right intervals and the right temperature, prompting the seeds to germinate. Then, in one brief burst of life, the plant sprouts, flowers, and goes to seed.

By far the most successful of desert plants here is the creosote. Immense plains of creosote cover the desert floor. In spring the bushes break out in a riot of blossoms that tinge the desert a gentle yellow. Year-round, except during severe drought, the bush remains verdant, its small, resinous leaves changing from vibrant green to olive drab with the whims of the weather.

More than 700 species of flowering plants grow in the region and most of them employ defenses that keep wildlife—and knowledgeable people— at a distance. Catclaw acacia seems to slash out with ferocious talons to tear at clothes and skin. The Mojave yucca, a large rosette of bayonet-shaped leaves, has stabbed more than one photographer who was stepping back for just the right composition.

"The Mojave is a desert where two other deserts meet," said Roger Alexander, a Bureau of Land Management natural resource specialist. "To the south is the Sonoran, a low, hot desert; to the north is the Great Basin, a high, cold desert. And the Mojave falls in between." We were on our way to the New York Mountains, one of the scenic area's highest ranges.

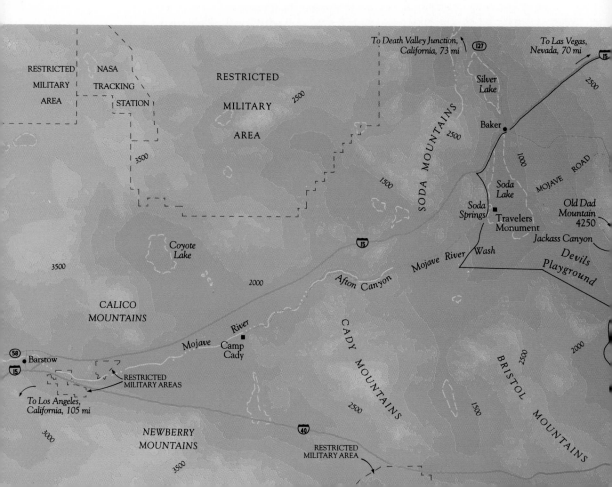

Approaching the New Yorks through sage and desert scrub oak, we took the four-wheel-drive as far as we could up an old mining road, then started hiking through rising forests of piñon and juniper. Rock tailings, vibrant with blues and greens, indicated that copper had once been mined here. I knelt for a closer look and picked out a piece of pyrite, fool's gold. Then I found a small amethyst. By the time we left this fine rockhounding spot, my knapsack and pockets bulged.

As we neared the top, the temperature dropped. Old-man cactus, grayed and whiskered, poked from lichen-covered rocks. The Christmassy scent of evergreens perfumed the air. Majestic white firs towered above us.

"White firs need 20 to 30 inches of water a year," Roger said. "These grow here because of the relatively cool temperatures and high level of moisture at this elevation. The mountains create their own weather. Even on the hottest summer day there's some moisture in the air, and as air rises up the sides of the mountains, it condenses into thunderheads. You'll be sitting in the valleys, dry as a bone, and look up to see huge black clouds raining down on the mountains."

From low, sun-scorched valleys to evergreen-shaded peaks more than 7,000 feet high, California's eastern Mojave Desert displays a diversity of ecosystems. The 1.5-million-acre East Mojave National Scenic Area encompasses 26 named mountain ranges as well as cinder cones, dry lakes, oases, and sand dunes.

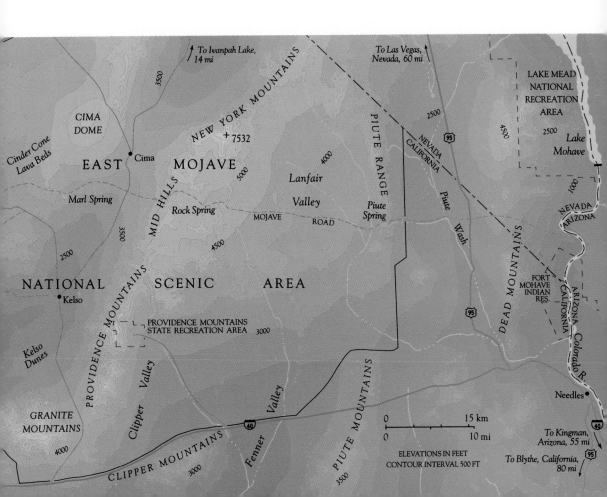

High on the mountains of the Mojave live bobcats, deer, and desert bighorn sheep—animals that could not thrive as well in the heat and aridity of the low desert. One day, while hiking in the Piute Range, I had the luck to see bighorn. North America's rarest big-game animal, the desert bighorn is legally hunted at two sites within the East Mojave National Scenic Area. For more than 100 years hunting of the bighorn was prohibited in California.

A ram with elegant curled horns perched on a rock cliff, alongside a ewe and a yearling. Curious and cautious, they watched me as closely as I watched them. The ram boldly ventured to the creek for water. Then all three bounded up the cliffs and disappeared.

I soon found myself adapting to desert ways, stocking up on water, seeking shade, avoiding the heat of day. This behavior is second nature to people who live in the desert. Many must also adapt to a life without running water, electricity, or telephones. They come for solitude. Finding cities and towns too crowded and too confining, they choose to live away from the rest of the world. Loners, yes; unfriendly, no.

The sign at Carl Faber's house says *Rock House* and *Come on up.* Carl, an artist and self-proclaimed desert rat, has lived in the Mojave 16 years. "I used to regard myself as a hermit," he told me. "For the first seven years I lived in complete solitude. Living alone for as long as I did made me appreciate people more. Now I'm real sociable. I encourage people to stop by."

Carl lives on a hill in a one-story rock structure that fits as naturally into the environment as a cactus or a yucca. Lured by the sign, people stop by to chat, to drop off books, extra firewood or water, and to see Carl's latest paintings.

"I don't have a gallery or an agent. I sell my paintings right from my door," said Carl, a tall, lanky man of 50 with curly hair and a mustache. Working in acrylics, pen and ink, and colored pencil, he produces near-photographic renderings of desert landscapes. "I've become a part of the landscape myself," he says. "I've had coyotes walk up to me when I'm painting, and I've had birds land on my head. I know the intimacies of light and dark, the shadings of the seasons. I know the postures of plants and how they grow in relation to one another. It's subtle, but I see it because I've spent so much time sitting quietly in the desert and painting."

Carl paints when he feels like it or when he needs money. "By giving up the need for money," he says, "I've simplified my life. And what I've gained is time, time that allows me to do the things that I want to do. There are no schedules to follow here, no deadlines to meet. I read. I hike. Right now I'm teaching myself Gershwin and Fats Waller on the guitar. I can just enjoy the heck out of a day."

Time. It takes on new dimensions in the desert. It expands. It fills the empty vastness. It stretches to far horizons and then waits patiently for you to catch up.

The desert is the kind of place where you can sit for an hour or two just to watch the blooming of a jimsonweed. As the day departs and darkness descends, the hypnotic jimsonweed slowly unfurls its white trumpet-like flower. As it opens, the fragrance becomes stronger. Attracted by the scent, carpenter bees zoom to the flower and collect the pollen. A friend who has watched these large bees perform told of seeing them wallow about drunkenly, acting as if they were intoxicated.

In summer the days are quiet and long. Daytime temperatures can soar to 120°F in the valleys, where whirling dust devils spin through the scorching air. Dry lakes shimmer with blue pools, mirages caused as particles in the air bend light to reflect the sky.

When rains come, they put on thunderous shows, with pyrotechnics and rainbow finales arching over the mountains, the heart of the scenic area. Twenty-six ranges rise from the desert floor like island archipelagoes. They began to be formed 5 million years ago. The earth's crust may be pulling apart here, and the 30 or so minor faults in the area show this. As the mountains erode, debris fans out and fills the valleys, creating the topography seen today.

The Mojave is a geologist's paradise. Bare-bones geology, they call it. The naked earth shows all—faults, uplifts, and eruptions. I asked a geologist if he could describe the geologic history of the Mojave in 25 words or less. "I can explain it in one," he said. "Complex."

I spent much time in the mountains, especially the Granites, my favorites. Soaring white peaks in the distance, the Granites up close look like a chaotic, precariously balanced pile of boulders. The effect is a rolling, tumbling terrain, perfect for bouldering, a form of rock climbing that can be described as leaping, crawling, and scrambling over rocks. It takes a focused mind, a flexible body, and faith. Often I had to rely on scant handholds and footholds. Sometimes I had to jump and hope I'd make it. And there were times when I found myself stuck and I had to figure a way out. Bouldering, I discovered, exercises both the body and the mind.

One afternoon while bouldering in the Granites I spied a pair of chuckwallas. Like all reptiles, the plump, rock-dwelling lizard is cold-blooded and raises its body temperature by absorbing heat from the sun's rays, the air, and rock surfaces. Throughout the day the chuckwalla makes constant adjustments, moving in or out of the shade to keep within a few degrees of its optimum body temperature.

I crept up for a closer look. The male pumped up and down, doing push-ups as a reptilian way of saying, "This is my territory. Keep out." For fear of scaring them away, I heeded his warning and retreated to watch from a distance. The chuckwalla is the largest of some 20 species of lizards that inhabit the Mojave; the male can grow to a length of 18 inches. Through nine-power binoculars he looked big enough to eat Tokyo.

Indians, who considered the chuckwalla a delicacy, fashioned a tool for capturing the lizard, which, when frightened, wedges itself into a rock crevice and gulps air to puff up like a balloon. Armed with a barbed pole, Indians punctured the inflated chuckwalla and pulled it from its crevice.

Archaeologists are not certain about when the Mojave was first inhabited, but stone tools give evidence of human presence about 12,000 years ago, around the end of the last ice age. Later, Indians left behind strange and mysterious rock art—thousands of human or animal figures, suns or planets, geometric or abstract designs. The strongest evidence suggests that the symbols marked springs, trails, and territorial claims. Pictures of animals may have been made by a shaman to invoke hunting magic. The real meaning of rock art may never be known, for the identity of the artisans has blown away on the winds.

Chemehuevi and Mojave Indians living in the desert when white men first came did not know who had created the rock art. Nomadic hunters and gatherers, the Chemehuevis roamed the Mojave in loosely knit family groups. The Mojaves were an agricultural tribe.

"Mojaves lived on the banks of the Colorado River. Each spring, when the river flooded, they planted crops of corn, melons, and squash," desert historian Dennis Casebier told me. "With time to travel, they traded with other tribes. The most important trade route was the one that went to the Pacific, where they bartered for shells with coastal Indians. When white men first came to the desert in the late 1770s, they asked the Mojaves to guide them, and this was the route they chose."

We had gathered our caravan of four-wheel-drives on the banks of the Colorado River to begin a three-day journey along the Mojave Road. As we headed west across the river's sandy floodplain, Dennis broadcast over a CB radio, relating the history of the trail. It had followed a route from spring to spring, each a day's travel from the next. The first spring, Piute, fed a creek, a green ribbon that winds through an isolated canyon in the Piute Range.

"By 1863, when Arizona became a territory, there was heavy traffic along the Mojave Road," Dennis said, standing beside the cool water of the creek. "Stagecoaches, immigrant trains, and mail wagons traveled the road, but mostly it was used by military wagon trains bringing supplies eastward to the new territory of Arizona. It would not be uncommon to see 300 soldiers and 500 to 600 animals camped out here."

From Piute Spring the original road rounds the treacherously steep Piute Range. Ruts cut by the rims of wagon wheels are still visible in the red volcanic rock. "It's an extremely difficult pass. Wagon trains had to double-team their mules," Dennis told us. "They devised an emergency brake by trailing a long log behind each wagon. When the mules tired and couldn't go any farther, the log would prevent the wagon from rolling too far back down the hill. I tell people to avoid this part of the trail. They'll do damage to their vehicle, to themselves, and to the environment." We took a short detour along powerline roads.

Through nearly twenty years of research, Dennis and a crew of desert rats known as the Friends of the Mojave Road have retraced the original trail, rebuilding it in places. In 1983 it was opened as an interpretive and recreational road. "It gives you a chance to experience the desert the way the Indians, the Army, cattlemen, and stagecoach passengers saw it," said Dennis. "The Mojave is a natural and cultural museum, and the Mojave Road is an eight-foot-wide, 138-mile-long artifact."

The sun-drenched plains of Lanfair Valley stretched before us, a landscape more garden than desert. Buckhorn cholla, Mojave yucca, cheeseweed, and creosote grew in profusion. A covey of quail dashed across the road. Jackrabbits darted in front of the vehicles. A few scattered homestead cabins broke the horizon.

Our next stop was Rock Spring, a trickle hemmed by high walls marked with Indian petroglyphs and military graffiti: *Stuar 4th Inf May 16.* The soldier was probably Charles Stuart of the California Volunteers, who had been here on May 16 in both 1863 and 1864. We lunched tailgate style, as did the wagon trains of Stuart's day. Our train was small, only four vehicles, but it made for manageable travel and close, friendly company.

We made camp on a hillside that overlooked a field of cinder cones, remnants of volcanic eruptions, one as recent as 330 years ago. The setting, cloaked in a hazy sunset, seemed prehistoric. We huddled around a campfire, regularly adding wood to keep the fire blazing. Nights in the desert can be cold, even in summer.

After a warming breakfast of French toast and hot chocolate, we broke camp. "Boots and saddles!" yelled Dennis to muster the troops. He took us down Jackass Canyon on an earlier route of the Mojave Road. As we passed the massive flanks of Old Dad Mountain, the great golden expanses of the Devils Playground spread before us. I had finally made it. The Playground was a peaceful place of sand-draped rolling hills, a place where time seemed to stand still. It was worth the wait.

In the distance we could see the startling whiteness of Soda Lake, its cracked surface bleached by alkaline salts and sodas. Near a spring-fed oasis at the western edge of the lake we came upon a cairn that stood six feet tall and was about twenty feet in diameter. Indians who traveled the desert marked trail intersections and other important places with piles of stones, potsherds, or seashells. In a more recent tradition, Dennis and his friends started raising a Travelers Monument, marking it with a brass plaque that only those who travel the road are privileged to read. We each added a rock to the growing pile.

"From here on, the road follows the riverbed of the Mojave River," Dennis said. "It's a strange river, a very poorly behaved one. It's larger at its headwaters than at its mouth. It doesn't drain to the ocean, but runs into the middle of the desert and stops. And most of the time it flows underground."

The Mojave River appears above the ground only after heavy rains or where rock formations force it to the surface. We followed the dry riverbed through Afton Canyon. Chiseled spires rose 500 feet in muted shades of pink, red, orange, and gray. When we finally came upon a stream of water, I waded across the Mojave River in two steps.

From here the route leaves public lands and passes through private property. We were at the end of our journey. We had spent three days on the Mojave Road, though our trip seemed much longer, as if we had traveled through time.

"There's plenty of time in the desert," Carl Faber had told me. "Plenty of time if you want it." For those willing to find that time, the desert will reveal its beauty, its mysteries, and its magic.

FOLLOWING PAGES: *Timeless forces of wind and water shape the Mojave. Kelso Dunes, formed over millennia and touched by fresh footprints, glows in day's late light. Beyond, a cloudburst's lightning stabs the Providence Mountains.*

147

In a sudden torrent perilous to the unwary, a flash flood engulfs a wash (opposite). Weather changes quickly in the desert, as cloudless blue skies abruptly darken and pour down black veils of rain. During summer months, thunderstorms may drop several inches of rain in an hour. Spring showers prompt plants such as the desert senna (below) to bloom. But the desert's scant rains— typically, six to eight inches a year—often get canceled out by heat and drying winds that rob moisture from the Mojave's perennially parched environment.

"Violent
summer
storms...
send flash
floods
roaring
down
the mountains."

Rain and rainbow hover on the mountain skyline while a thirsty earth waits.
Clumps of big galleta grass help to anchor ever-shifting Kelso Dunes.

FOLLOWING PAGES: Buckhorn cholla and creosote flourish among the boulders of
Granite Mountains, providing habitat for a variety of desert creatures.

Oblivious to a sticky situation, a white-tailed antelope ground squirrel (opposite) nibbles on a buckhorn cholla, source of nutrients and vital moisture. Nearly 300 species of animals inhabit the Mojave, each adapted to endure extremes of heat and aridity. A jackrabbit (below) browses on creosote leaves. Oversize ears radiate heat from its body. The desert tortoise (lower) stores water in sacs beneath its shell. Picked up, it reacts by jettisoning its water reserve.

157

Racing with the wind, a landsailer skims across the cracked surface of Ivanpah Lake (opposite). Sailers and crew (below) ready their "dirt boats" for the annual Ivanpah Regatta. Lightweight wheeled shells with a single sail, landsailers can attain speeds of up to 90 miles per hour as the driver zips along only inches above the ground. "It's not a bumpy ride at all," says Dwight Cope, a former national landsailing champion. "It's incredibly smooth and quiet." The Bureau of Land Management has set aside part of the lake for such recreation. Regulations barring motorized vehicles keep the surface unscarred for the landsailers.

Symbol of the Mojave, Joshua trees form eerie figures at twilight. At dusk, the desert grows busy with the traffic of nocturnal animals. Owls fly on silent wings, scorpions creep across the desert floor, and menageries of rodents hop about like windup toys. Kit fox cubs (opposite, upper) emerge from an underground den; they'll hunt in the cool of the evening. A night-prowling ringtail (opposite, lower) slips out of a rock crevice. Prospectors kept ringtails to catch rats and mice.

FOLLOWING PAGES: Sunlight softly strokes the rolling sands of the Devils Playground. The Mojave, an ageless land, preserves the solitude of wilderness, the grandeur of sky upon mountain, and the sorcery of the desert.

CRAIG AURNESS / WEST LIGHT

"Its beauty,
      its mysteries,
  and its magic."

JONATHAN S. BLAIR (ABOVE, BELOW, AND FOLLOWING PAGES)

By James Raffan

Photographs by Richard Alexander Cooke III

Enchanted River

Canadian Odyssey on Waters Clear and Wild

Amid rippling reflections of aptly named Clearwater Lake, a laden canoe embarks on a voyage through l'Eau Claire wilderness in subarctic Quebec.

Picture a red canoe floating on water so clear that the boat seems suspended between lush earth and mackerel sky. Its symmetrical shadow, projecting through six feet of water, darkens the pink granite below. Upstream, a trout twists, startled by the canoe. Ahead, the river's smooth-water horizon is broken by glistening sparks flung from a rapid below.

This is Rivière à l'Eau Claire in northern Quebec—the enchanted Clearwater River, flowing through the transition between boreal forest and tundra, between Indian and Inuit territory, and beyond the smudge of industry. Its waters nourish a hidden wilderness sanctuary on the east shore of Hudson Bay, one of the most remote parts of North America.

That idyllic scene is gone for now, replaced in my mind by concentration on the scouted route. The loaded canoe feels fat and unresponsive in the wild water. I tighten my life vest and press my knees against the sides. My partner, John Fallis, turns in the bow and asks, "You all set?" I nod, tingling with anticipation.

Sliding over the first tongue is a strangely calm and uncomplicated event. Then converging three-foot waves jostle the canoe and launch us headlong into the exhilarating wash and foam of the rapid. The bow rises and drives deep. We take on water. John yells, "We'd better head for that eddy!" We touch the eddy, and as if in the hands of some riparian imp, the bow of the boat is whirled upstream. Driven by eddy water rushing counter to the main current, the stern rotates, a maneuver that combines the rush of a power stop on snow skis and the delicious caprice of a roller coaster. It is a wet and wild beginning to our remote river expedition.

Weeks before, to get the trip under way, photographer Rik Cooke and I teamed up with John Fallis, Ontario naturalist, outdoor educator, and seasoned wilderness canoeist, with whom I had paddled many of Canada's northern rivers. The three of us joined Mark Scriver, inscrutable guide, packhorse, and gourmand, chosen by reputation to outfit our difficult expedition.

We had all met together for the first time at Black Feather Wilderness Adventures in Ottawa, which outfitted the expedition. (We had shipped the canoes ahead.) The Black Feather packing room was hot and rich with the smells of leather, varnish, dried food, tents, and old campfires.

All of this gear—922 pounds of packs and waterproofed barrels—had to go by jet to Great Whale River, a community of 1,300 people on the east coast of Hudson Bay, and then northeast 146 miles by floatplane to Lac à l'Eau Claire. Even locating the town of Great Whale River on our maps was a challenge; it might be called Kuujjuarapik (its official Inuit name), Whapmagoostui (Cree), or, on French maps, Poste-de-la-Baleine.

We launched the expedition with what we had expected to be an eight-hour flight. But Canada's unpredictable northern weather held up our departure for four days. Experts have an explanation for what repeatedly trapped us at airports: Cold wind comes in from over the pack ice in Hudson Bay and runs into warm air over the land, creating dense fog.

Weather has played a significant role in keeping this area wild. After Henry Hudson's voyage of discovery into the bay in 1610, the quests for a northwest passage focused attention on the western shore of Hudson Bay.

Most trading posts were built there, despite rumors of great bounty and a route to fur riches in Labrador through l'Eau Claire wilderness. Ice and treacherous weather kept the Eastmain—the east coast of Hudson Bay—virtually untouched by the ships of white explorers.

Native people have lived near the mouth of the Clearwater River for centuries. White settlers have been few. The Hudson's Bay Company established a small post at the Richmond Gulf in 1750. Shortly afterward, it closed for lack of business. Today's cultural blend of natives and whites got its start in 1955. In that year a control center for the Pinetree Line, a Canadian-U.S. early warning defense system, was established at Great Whale River.

The weather finally broke, and our flight from Montreal landed in a flurry of dust on the gravel strip at Great Whale River. We located our canoes, one nested inside the other for shipping, on the top rack of an airport warehouse. We then moved all our gear to the Center for Northern Studies, where we made preparations for the last leg.

Serge Payette, the center's senior scientist, told us just how undeveloped and remote l'Eau Claire wilderness is. "There's nobody living there. If the Inuit and Cree maintain their tendency to go there to hunt, thereby maintaining their claim to the land, it will be virgin area in the future." Payette's words were understated compared with those of Craig Macdonald, Canadian historian and adventurer, who, after a winter trek said, "It is a formidable, terrifying, harsh type of land—an order of magnitude better than any place I've been before."

My first impression of l'Eau Claire wilderness had come from reading about a 1938 expedition in search of an elusive freshwater seal, which the Inuit of Hudson Bay called *kasagea*. The expedition hired a Cree Indian, Daniel Petagumskum, to guide the party up the coast from Great Whale River to the Richmond Gulf, overland to Lac à l'Eau Claire, and beyond to Lacs des Loups Marins, where two of the seals were found.

At Great Whale River, to my delight, I met Petagumskum's grandson Elijah, a stocky chap with a broad smile. He was working as an apprentice electrician for the local fuel company. When I asked him about his grandfather, his eyes lit up. "But," he said, "I am not the one who should be telling you about this because I have lived most of my life here in Great Whale River. Why not come and talk to my father-in-law, because he used to live and hunt up that way, too. I will translate for you."

Matthew George, 72 years old, sat at his kitchen table with his hands folded neatly on a plastic tablecloth. Speaking through Elijah, he said he had lived for a time at the Richmond Gulf and that each August, in the 1930s and 1940s, his family traveled upriver to Lac à l'Eau Claire to fish and hunt caribou. If the hunting was good, they would return in early December. But often they would live in tents in the heart of the interior for the entire winter, returning when the ice began breaking up.

With topographic maps spread across his living room carpet, Matthew pointed, laughed, and talked. His wife, Mina, who is ten years younger than Matthew, added her recollections. Matthew and Mina reminisced in their native Cree; Elijah interrupted every now and then in English.

"My mother died of tuberculosis and we buried her here," Matthew

167

said, pointing to an island in Lac à l'Eau Claire. "After that, we hunted in other places. Some years, you were lucky; some years, you were not. If you don't kill anything, no food. In 1929, Miyaeino and his family, six of them, starved to death on this island at the outlet of the river because they had no strength to catch more food. They tried to catch fish. His brother even went to the next lake to try to catch a seal, but they ran out of food."

Matthew's stories gripped me. We had packs full of wholesome trail food that Mark would cook into gourmet meals. We would have chocolate fondue, spaghetti escargot, fresh lake trout, quiche, and hummus with crumbled Danish blue cheese and sprouts. Getting ready to leave Matthew's house, I heard our floatplane swoop over the village. I ran down to the dock to begin the loading, with these tales of starvation and hardship—endured by people in the exact place we were going—adding their weight to my mental store of expectations and apprehensions.

Guy Lampron, the pilot of our de Havilland Single Otter, looked every bit the Canadian bush pilot with his scuffed boots, scarlet flying suit, and thick black mustache. Though he allowed us to help load the nested canoes onto the port pontoon and to heft the gear into the cabin, Guy was the last one to secure each item. Simply by boarding this aging workhorse—our Otter had been in service almost 30 years—we became part of a northern Canadian tradition. The radial engine roared and we were off. After the stratospheric detachment of a commercial jet, I welcomed the

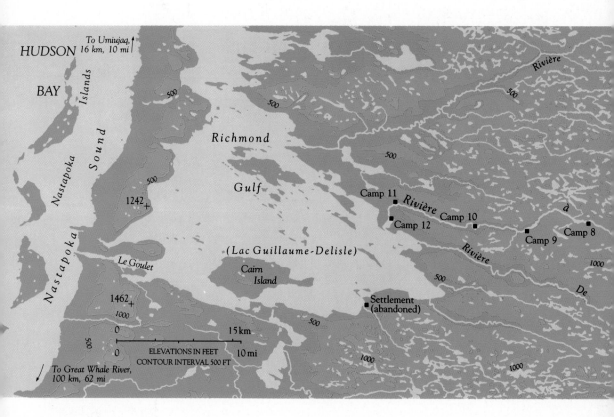

change of flying at 90 knots and 1,400 feet in the noisy old Otter. Everything below seemed so close, so clear. To the west, the pack ice of Hudson Bay, the domain of seals, beluga whales, and polar bears; to the east were the bare, mineral-rich ridges of the continent's bedrock, the Canadian Shield. Trees, mostly conifers—white spruce, black spruce, and tamarack—grew in sheltered valleys. And on the north-facing slopes, drifts of snow still clung to the green landscape on this sunny July day.

Guy nudged my arm. Unable to be heard over the roar of the engine, he pointed ahead and then to a map on his knee, drawing my attention to a rocky promontory protecting the triangular gulf from the wild waters of Hudson Bay. This was one of the features that gave planners reason to designate the region a Natural Area of Canadian Significance, a low-ranking recognition on the way to possible national park status.

We dropped from the sky through a shadowed landscape, drenched in the long yellow light of evening, and landed on the stillness of Lac à l'Eau

Remote and pristine, the wilderness called l'Eau Claire lies about 750 miles due north of Ottawa—with the nearest road link 150 miles to the south. A band of the Canadian Shield spanning the 56th parallel, l'Eau Claire separates Cree and Inuit, forest and tundra. On the Rivière à l'Eau Claire canoe route, modern voyageurs must cope with bloodthirsty insects and formidable portages.

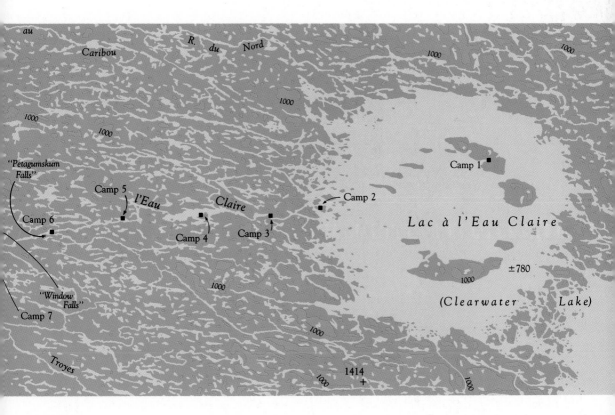

Claire. The lake reflected island edges and the dreamy, white-patterned filigree of a blue northern sky. No boats, no people, no signs of civilization whatsoever. Just rocks and trees. In traditional Québécois style, we called, *"Merci beaucoup, Guy! Salut!"* And with that the Otter's engine roared and then faded into the stillness, leaving us on the island where Matthew George's mother, Maggie, was buried.

That evening I sat in the quiet and marveled at how lucky we were to enter a world uncomplicated by human beings. It was as though the Otter had magically transported us from the foggy world of airports and combustion engines to a shining clean and quiet place where a simpler life prevailed. Our schedule would be the schedule of the wind; we would travel when the weather allowed; we would eat when we were hungry; we would sleep when we were tired.

Shelter, warmth, nourishment, and rest now would be everyday priorities. We had been transported with our canoes into another land, one that would force us to confront our terrestrial, warm-blooded existence. We were in a world where the forces of nature, for a change, would reacquaint us with our fallibility.

Next morning, John and I walked to the other side of the island, to the burial place described by Matthew George. A piquant combination of sun-warmed mushroom and musk wavered in the still air as we walked through luxuriant, ankle-deep lichens called caribou moss. We came to a sandy beach and followed the prints of a black bear cub. They led us to a place where ax scars on tree stumps and a curious orientation of lichen-encrusted pegs marked a piece of ground about grave size. We felt that we had found the spot where Maggie George had been buried nearly four decades before.

The bear tracks continued, and I followed for no particular reason, feeling strangely numinous. In my mind's eye, I saw a canvas tent secured to the snow by taut hemp guy lines, a wobbly smokestack sticking through a hole in the tent's roof, rich woodsmoke cutting the winter air, and a caribou carcass hanging near the door. Matthew and his father were silently tending nets on the lake ice, while Matthew's new wife, Mina, ministered to her dying mother-in-law.

When we set out on the wild river, this spell, cast by the land and its people, was broken. At that first rapid, when we went ashore to scout a route through the haystacks, rocks, and rip currents, the flies came. Our brightly colored parkas slowly darkened with thousands of blackflies. A swipe of the hand across exposed flesh would reduce countless hundreds of them to a fishy-smelling black cream.

Mark, who was without his bug hat, suddenly yelled "Arrrrghhh!" and bolted. When we finally caught up with him out on the river, he explained, "It was getting difficult to breathe!"

Blackflies, mosquitoes, and horseflies were there in numbers to confound the imagination. From inside the tent, their constant bumping on the outside often sounded like rain. Scientists reckon that populations of some mosquito species may reach five million to the acre. Unfortunately for all creatures with blood, there are in the north some 70 species of mosquitoes and more than 100 species of blackflies.

A large number of bites can produce a severe reaction that causes hands, ears, and faces to swell and itch. While scratching my hands on any exposed Velcro strip, and batting ears that felt like partially inflated inner tubes, I had to remind myself that suffering is a necessary element of a wilderness experience.

Rik fought back with a nightly massacre, killing the bugs inside his tent. From outside the tent the exercise looked like a man engaged in a vigorous wrestling match with a large python. But he was determined not to let them interfere with his general good humor or his job. He learned to drink through his bug hat and to operate his cameras with gloved hands.

Insects aside, ours was a world of green enchantment. The conifers were a deep chrome green, with vertical black bars where narrow trunks showed through sparse branches. Exposed sections of land emitted a dusty shade of pastel green, almost white at times, which derived from caribou moss. The occasional alder thickets were a lighter jade color. Completing the spectrum of this captivating, monochromatic world were strips of phosphorescent green perennials such as sedge and horsetail that edged streams and marshes.

To be part of this transitional landscape, born of long harsh winters and hurried summers, was to be swayed by its unity of color and its richness of plant and animal life. Sharing the calm pools on the river were eider ducks, scoters, and loons with young. Skittering along the shores were greater yellowlegs, sandpipers, and plovers. Even kingfishers and robins, both at the northern extent of their ranges, flew over the river from time to time. In the spruce groves, we could hear redpolls, chickadees, and dark-eyed juncos nesting in hidden places. On one rainy night, John, responding to the calling of a worried white-crowned sparrow, found a nest and four tiny fledglings sharing the shelter of our kitchen tarp.

As we made our way down the river toward the Richmond Gulf, we often saw raptors cruising the updrafts, seemingly startled off their cliffside aeries by the passing canoes. Golden eagles and feisty little merlins stayed high and away from the water. Ospreys, though, often came close overhead, to dive before our eyes and rise with a white-bellied fish—perhaps a speckled trout—in their claws.

One day John spied a renegade member of the 600,000-strong George River caribou herd. Blending with the muted brown hues of the shore, he stood defiantly, a bull from one of the world's largest herds. The animal flung its massive antlered head from side to side and scratched with its hind feet, the way a dog might, first one flank and then the other.

As Rik and Mark paddled to within 100 yards, the caribou froze and stared, as if unable to make sense of the approaching red apparition. The caribou then had another quick scratch and trotted off down the shore. Suddenly, it stopped, turned, and charged toward Rik and Mark, who were nearly beached. The bull turned again just before reaching them and crashed up the steep valley wall through a tangle of alder. "All I saw were these antlers, running right toward my lens," Rik told us. "Before I knew it, it was too close to focus!"

However captivating the wildlife might be, we were always conscious of white-water obstacles. The upper third of Rivière à l'Eau Claire was a blend of short, steep, and runnable rapids, interspersed with sections of flat water with current that ran at a persistent 3 to 5 miles per hour. Most of the 780-foot vertical drop of the river, however, was expended on a series of stunning waterfalls.

Although one cataract was marked on the map as having a drop of 315 feet (nearly twice that of Niagara), this, in reality, turned out to be a series of smaller drops, the greatest of which was about 70 feet. These falls meant many, many portages.

There were no portage trails. Matthew George had explained that the Cree used to get from the Richmond Gulf to Lac à l'Eau Claire by paddling and portaging up the imposing vertical drop of Rivière à l'Eau Claire. But, at some time early in the 20th century, someone found an easier route that used the valley of the Rivière De Troyes, one watershed south. Had l'Eau Claire been a historical route even in the last six or seven decades, there would have been well-established portage routes around all of the rapids and falls. As it was, because very few canoe parties have gone down the river, we had to bushwhack our way around all water obstacles.

On days when the weather was cool and the wind kept the bugs at bay, portaging was hellishly hard work; on those days when dead insects and sweat combined to make our skin crawl and our eyes burn, l'Eau Claire was a portaging challenge of legendary difficulty. But, no matter how hard the carry, the splendors of crashing water recompensed in full.

Because these magnificent natural phenomena are nameless, we took it upon ourselves to give them working titles. At "Petagumskum Falls," where we memorialized guide Daniel, we set up our tents high above plunging water. The campsite provided a different vista in every direction: To the north, the rapids led up to the falls, with a backdrop of deeply dissected hills; to the east, another veed river valley met l'Eau Claire. Westward, the clear water that we had yet to paddle stretched into the distance. And, to the south, the falls lay shrouded in wet, rainbowed mist.

The next morning we saw nothing but fog—cold, wet fog that ripped and tingled on the tip of a wicked northwest wind. By now inured to weather conditions and bugs that challenged his patience, Rik looked back at his tent, nearly turned inside out by the gale, and said in a droll voice, "Guys, I think my tent is trying to give birth to a hang glider!"

We laughed, tacitly acknowledging the bond of shared adversity. When conditions were miserable, we were no longer guide, naturalist, photographer, and writer; we were trail companions, bonded to each other, to the land and, in a tangible way now, to Matthew and his people. And this land, this inexorable teacher, still had plans for us.

Always, when approaching a major rapid or falls we heard the sound of the menace before we saw it. As we drifted closer, this falls sounded different. At one moment we would hear the lash of pounding water; the next minute the sound would diminish to a benign rumble. The map notation sounded innocuous: simply "Portage two miles." And so began an eight-hour carry.

After about an hour of humping canoes and pack loads through spruce groves, up hills, and through moss swamps and alder thickets, I was tired, and in a decidedly bad humor. Portaging is a lonely business; one that leaves each body part aching and the mind barraged with a pain-induced monologue: *Why did I end up with the food packs and all this loose stuff to carry? Never mind, just keep going. Why did I agree to do this, anyway? Shut up! You can go farther. That burning pain at the nape of my neck. And the bugs! Aiiiieeee! If only I'd studied Zen. . . .*

I emerged from a spruce and alder jungle high above the river, and all was forgotten. It took a moment or two to focus on the visual beauty, until now masked by those menacing sounds. Before me, green water was transformed into a white tumult that thundered into billows of wet mist rising out of a narrow canyon.

Off came my bug hat and shirt, and the most refreshing balm washed over my fly-stained face. I stood transfixed until the mist-spawned droplets ran down my skin. Agony and ecstasy merged; the magic of that cataract was made more powerful by the struggle to get there. It was a case of elemental extremes: first, hardship, then elation. One of the reasons for going to the wilderness is that there are no happy mediums.

We had lunch in the spray of the falls and carried on, totally refreshed. Uphill wandering on lichen-slippery slopes turned into downhill drudgery. Too tired to carry, we slid our loaded canoes over logs and rocks, down streambeds, until we became entangled in a jungle of alder growing in the bottom of our portaging valley.

Eight hours after starting, I dumped my last load on the shore and waded into the river. I knelt on a flat rock and immersed my head, opened my eyes, and began gulping. Swallow after swallow after swallow, the refreshing water penetrated and cooled. Head up, hair and beard dripping, I was struck by the simplicity of it all. At one time a person could quench a thirst in almost any stream on the continent. Now, only in pockets of wilderness like this one was it possible. Someday will there be no more "clearwater" rivers to drink from? Will anyone remember?

On the day after the long portage, it rained, a cold, all-day rain. Thankful for the rest, I lay in the tent in my sleeping bag and inhaled the smell of wet nylon and old sweat. And I stared at a familiar scene—the stains of a thousand smeared mosquitoes on the delicate, once-white nylon; I saw the seams, the slight rip in the door screening, the limp lines overhead where socks had dried overnight so many times. The land had bonded us to this portable home-away-from-home. It felt good to be there—to know the rain would pass and we would have strength to begin again: a last push to the Richmond Gulf.

The final obstacle, according to the maps, would be a stretch of rapids nearly two miles long, impossible for our loaded canoes, even with spray covers. But Mark said, "I'd like to get a good look at this last rapid to make sure that it can't be shot. I don't want to carry if we don't have to."

The river narrowed to a gorge as our canoes slipped with the current downstream from our campsite. We pulled into a back eddy at the outside of a sharp bend in the river, stepped up on the shore, and saw frenzied white water extending far beyond our vision. "There's no way we'll shoot that," Mark said, with a tone of resignation.

Six hours later, we completed the portage, again plagued by an alder jungle and insects. But at last we waded the canoes over tidal flats and took our first strokes in the saltwater of the Richmond Gulf.

After days of river adventure, the jubilation of our return to the sea was surprisingly muted. No triumphant feeling of victory overwhelmed us sitting there in the evening sunlight on the gulf. Instead, we experienced a feeling of gratitude to a land and a place that had taught us and humbled us with hard lessons. We felt communion, satisfaction, and success bestowed by and shared with a stern, yet benevolent, teacher.

The next day, Rik made his way up the bank of the river and into the gorge to photograph the river's last hurrah; Mark went on a long wood-gathering foray and then baked bread on the shore; John took a canoe and fished for arctic char in the estuary. Each of us in his own way was taking time to celebrate and reflect on a powerful encounter with a wild world. I treated myself to a climb up the ridge behind our campsite, where I mulled over the river trip and the history of this place.

I saw Cairn Island. There in 1750 Hudson's Bay Company Captains William Coats and Thomas Mitchell had established a trading post. Farther south, across water shadowed with currents and shoals, I could see the point where Matthew George and his family had lived before moving to Great Whale River.

In the distance was Le Goulet, the narrow water link to Hudson Bay, the unpredictable tidal danger zone that Mitchell had called the "Gulph of Hazard." History from my vantage point seemed more real than it ever had when I was reading the printed accounts, and, sitting there in the sunshine, I felt a part of history.

At about four o'clock that afternoon, I awoke from a nap on my windy ridge and saw in the distance a motor canoe snaking its way toward the river mouth through the myriad shoals of the Richmond Gulf. A group of four Inuit guides from Umiujaq, an Inuit community to the north, had come by prearrangement to show us around their gulf hunting grounds.

James Kasudluak watched me work my way down from the ridge. When we met, he said he sometimes walked inland over that ridge to hunt caribou. "Do you camp up there?" I asked. "Oh, no," he replied, with a grin. "That's what the Cree do. We always camp on the coast."

That statement reminded me that only white people regard this land as wilderness. It is the hunting ground of the Cree and Inuit, as it has been for centuries. Although many of the Cree and Inuit of the Eastmain live today in settlements with color TV, phones, kitchen appliances, and other 20th-century trappings, this land still gives them their identity, and it will in the future.

Our visit seemed complete only after we had a chance to meet and to talk with both Cree and Inuit users of the land. They are of that land as much as the caribou, the osprey, or the dusty green lichens. Isaac Anowak, the leader of the Inuit guide group, spoke of this belonging as he showed us around the gulf in his motor canoe. "I was born near here," he said, "and all my life I have been traveling around. I grew up in Great Whale. I spent time in Moosonee with tuberculosis. I went to high school and college in

Winnipeg, and I have worked in Salluit and Kuujjuaq for a total of about four years. But it wasn't until I moved to Umiujaq—to here at the Richmond Gulf—that I felt at home."

That this coastal place is home for Isaac, and not for white or Cree people, is reflected in the names each has given to the channel linking the Richmond Gulf to the main body of Hudson Bay. Captain William Coats wrote, "The Indians shew us their wisdom on divers occasions, and in none more than in their choice of names of creatures and places, which always imply something of their nature and quality."

The name for Mitchell's Gulph of Hazard echoes *Qua-qua-chich-i-uan*, a Cree word for the narrows, which means "it swallows quickly." But Isaac, in the tradition of his coastal people, called the channel *tuksuruq*, which simply means "porch." He explained: "If you imagine the whole Richmond Gulf as a tent, tuksuruq is the place you would enter."

Isaac wants to share his homeland with other people. As a tourism idea, he would fix up the old settlement on the south shore of the Gulf, where Matthew George and his family lived until 1954, as a "period village." Isaac's plans seem sensitive to the nature of the place, and represent a new thrust to build an economic base consistent with both 20th-century realities and traditional native values.

Wildernesses like l'Eau Claire often come to be regarded as sacred spaces, where life is under the elemental governance of fire and air, river and rock. Wilderness expands interior boundaries, enhancing one's capacity to be, to think, and to feel. This expedition reminded me that my southern Ontario home and all other urban places once were wilderness.

Going to the wilderness returns you to a time when fire was the great catalyst of conversation and retrospection; to a time when air was clean; to a time when fish could swim with the rhythm of the river's pulses and not with the throbbing beat of a hydroelectric generator; to a time when rock could be appreciated for its geologic and aesthetic appeal and not just its mineral potential. A return to the wilderness acquaints you with challenges that technology cannot ignore, with a place that has the power to humble the proudest of people.

Wild wind and waves came up. We could not, as planned, travel to Umiujaq with Isaac's party. Now, dozing in my tent and listening to the wind, I heard Charlie Anowak, Isaac's nephew, on the native radio channel, speaking in a musical cadence, *"Kuu-jju-ara'mut, Kuu-jju-ara'mut: Tasiura'mit, Tasiura'mit: Atai!"*—"Great Whale River, Great Whale River: this is Richmond Gulf, Richmond Gulf: over!" Using the combination of Charlie's efforts and our radio link to the Center for Northern Studies, we managed, eventually, to get a floatplane to come to pick us up. I wondered if the spirit of the land just wanted us to wait a little longer.

Finally, the drone of a floatplane drifted our way on the wind. Our link to the other world was coming. Soon Isaac and his companions would be gone, and we would be on our way home, leaving the landscape the way it was. But I would have a lifetime's worth of mindscape memories, blowing like a fresh northern wind across images of my southern world, re-forming them into what they once had been.

Following a ribbon of blue through a harshly beautiful land (opposite), the author's plane heads for Clearwater Lake. A Canadian prospector once called such wilds "the toughest country I ever saw." The canoe trip begins on the lake (below) with pilot Guy Lampron supervising the unloading of the party's gear. The author secures the plane while guide Mark Scriver unloads a recycled, waterproofed barrel. The nested canoes made the flight lashed to a pontoon.

"We dropped
    from the sky
  through
    a shadowed
  landscape."

"Headlong into the exhilarating wash and foam of the rapid."

Naturalist John Fallis catapults through a mountain of water—technically, a Class III haystack—that douses his partner, the author. Blue straps secure a nylon spray cover to rope loops on the flexible plastic hull. Waves roil not because of rocks but from the collision of a fast-flowing tongue and the waters of a slower pool. In the same rapid (opposite) paddlers hurtle past a black spruce forest and outcroppings covered with lichens, blueberries, and dwarf birches.

FOLLOWING PAGES: Sunrise paints a pastel backdrop for an ancient stage of stone and spruce. Huge glacial erratics, also known as perched blocks, support venerable lichens. The Labrador ice sheet bore the rocks west 7,000 years ago.

Evening at Camp 5 (below) brings on the ritual of fire-building in a metal firebox, used to prevent scarring of the ground. John stokes with twigs of heat-rich spruce while Mark prepares soup, cabbage salad, and pudding—accompaniments to a four-pound lake trout (right) caught at lunch. Barbless lures, eight-pound line, and a little luck will catch a meal from large populations of speckled trout, lake trout, and, near the coast, arctic char.

FOLLOWING PAGES: *Nameless spectacle, dubbed "Window Falls" by the author's party, churns the waters near Camp 7. Pleistocene ice, exploiting a fault in the rock, probably caused the original depression that fostered these channels.*

Dawn's light at Camp 9 softens torrent and mist. Later in that glorious morning (opposite, lower), sun and spray bestow a private rainbow upon Mark's canoe.

FOLLOWING PAGES: *Arc of spruce, rooted in a fault, rises behind John and Jim as they prepare to shoot a rapid. Post-glacial waters scoured the walls of this canyon on the lower l'Eau Claire, leaving the river to drop in steps to Hudson Bay.*

187

"Blackflies, mosquitoes,
and horseflies...
in numbers to
confound the imagination."

*Taking a break past the journey's halfway point, John (with pack) and Jim
discuss tactics on the toughest l'Eau Claire portage, an eight-hour ordeal. Under
duress of heat, exhaustion, and blackflies, they choose to lower loaded canoes by
rope (opposite) through a tangled forest of spruce, willow, and alder. Nylon head
nets and repellent-soaked outer clothing keep hungry insects at bay.*

Canoe toters walk across lush tundra beside a nameless 90-foot fall. Because of the river's many falls and treacherous rapids, Cree hunters avoided it, taking a more southerly route to caribou hunting grounds at Clearwater Lake.

Caught by camera flash in 10 p.m. twilight, constellations of insects buzz weary cooks at Camp 10 (below). Later, the aurora borealis glows over Isaac Anowak's patched tent on the Richmond Gulf (opposite). Science explains the northern lights as energized solar particles making atmospheric atoms glow. The Inuit saw the rippling lights as their white-clad ancestors, dancing in the dark. Another sky myth transformed a star cluster—the Pleiades—into a flock of doves. Here the doves rise just above the horizon, gracing an enchanted sky afire with the beauty and the power, the wonder and the peace, of the wilderness.

Notes on Contributors

THOMAS B. ALLEN, a former member of the National Geographic Society staff, is the author or co-author of several books, including the recently published *Merchants of Treason* and *War Games*. He is also the author of Special Publications' *Vanishing Wildlife of North America* and wrote a chapter for *America's Outdoor Wonders*. Tom and his wife, Scottie, live in Bethesda, Maryland.

CRAIG AURNESS, who specializes in capturing the images of the American West, has photographed eight articles for NATIONAL GEOGRAPHIC. Books featuring his images include *Iowa, The American Heartland, The West, Los Angeles/Hollywood,* and *California.* Craig, who lives in Los Angeles, is one of the founders of West Light, a photographic agency that represents 50 professional photographers.

TOM BEAN, educated in wildlife biology, was a National Park Service ranger in Death Valley, California; Wind Cave National Park in South Dakota, and Glacier Bay National Park and Preserve in Alaska. A free-lancer since 1982, he has a special interest in photographing parklands and wilderness landscapes. His photographs have appeared in TRAVELER and will appear in Special Publications' forthcoming *Excursions to Enchantment.* Tom lives near Flagstaff, Arizona.

JONATHAN S. BLAIR, a contract photographer for the Society, began his National Geographic career in 1967 after a stint as a National Park Service ranger. His many world-spanning assignments have taken him north of the Arctic Circle in search of migrating birds and down Ethiopia's Omo River in search of crocodiles. He has also aimed his camera at the sky to capture images of comets and meteors. He has a degree in photographic illustration from the Rochester Institute of Technology. Jonathan lives in Wilmington, Delaware.

RICHARD ALEXANDER COOKE III, a free-lance photographer, has covered such Special Publications assignments as *Canada's Wilderness Lands, America's Wild and Scenic Rivers, Exploring America's Valleys, Builders of the Ancient World,* and *America's Ancient Cities.* His photographs have appeared in such magazines as *Outside* and *Sports Afield.*

DAVID HISER has free-lanced for the Society since 1968. In addition to 20 stories for the GEOGRAPHIC, he has contributed to more than a dozen Special Publications books, including *The Mighty Aztecs, Blue Horizons,* and *Window on America.* His trip to the Lacandon Forest was his seventh journey to Mexico for the Society. He lives in Aspen, Colorado, where he is a member of Photographers/Aspen, a photographic cooperative.

GEORGE F. MOBLEY, a member of the National Geographic Society staff since 1961, has covered assignments from Alaska to Antarctica. A graduate of the University of Missouri School of Journalism, he worked for Air Force publications and as a free-lance writer and photographer before joining the Society staff. George lives with his wife, Marilyn, on a small farm on the Shenandoah River in Virginia.

JAMES RAFFAN has spent 25 years adventuring by canoe, snowshoe, dogsled, bicycle, and on foot. A former wilderness canoe guide, he is a member of the Queens University faculty of education. He has written about his expeditions in two recent books, *Wild Waters: Canoeing Canada's Wilderness Rivers* and *Canexus: The Canoe and Canoe Culture.*

CYNTHIA RUSS RAMSAY has written for more than a dozen Special Publications books, including *Nature on the Rampage, Splendors of the Past, Our Awesome Earth,* and *Alaska's Magnificent Parklands.* She has also served as managing editor of the Society's Books for Young Explorers.

PHILIP SCHERMEISTER, a free-lance photographer based in San Francisco, has covered several stories for WORLD magazine. He also contributed to *Window on America.* A graduate of the University of Minnesota, he was a news photographer for the Topeka *Capital-Journal* for five years.

SCOTT THYBONY, who lives in Flagstaff, Arizona, has frequently covered assignments in the Southwest for Society publications. Working as a writer, wilderness guide, and archaeologist, he has traveled to many remote areas of North America. A contributor to *Outside* and *National Wildlife* magazines, he is the author of *Fire and Stone,* a guide to Wupatki and Sunset Crater national monuments in Arizona.

SUZANNE VENINO joined the National Geographic Society staff in 1977 after graduating from George Washington University. As a staff writer for seven years, she wrote several children's books for the Society and contributed to several Special Publications books, including *America's Hidden Corners* and *Exploring America's Scenic Highways.* Now a free-lancer, she lives in Telluride, Colorado.

S. JEFFREY K. WILKERSON has spent 25 years in tropical research. From his investigations of Mexico's pre-Columbian cultures have come GEOGRAPHIC articles about the Totonacs and Huastecs in Veracruz and the development of the Usumacinta River, which forms part of the border between Mexico and Guatemala. Jeff also followed the route of Cortés for the GEOGRAPHIC. The author of *El Tajín, a Guide for Visitors* lives in Veracruz, Mexico.

MICHAEL S. YAMASHITA, a free-lance photographer based in New Jersey, roams the earth on assignments. His photographs have appeared in Special Publications' *Splendors of the Past, Majestic Island Worlds* and *Lakes, Peaks, and Prairies: Discovering the United States-Canadian Border,* for which he was the principal photographer.

Acknowledgments

The Special Publications Division gratefully acknowledges the assistance of the people named or quoted in the text and the following: Susan Alexander, F. W. Chandler, Harold G. Colt, Charles M. DeLorme, Lenore Hanson, Noah Inukpuk, Belinda Kaye, Don Keller, James E. Lothan, Georgina McCormack, James D. Nations, Kenneth S. Norris, Robert M. Norris, Wally Schaber, Shirlee Ann Smith, Terry R. Sopher, Alex D. VanHemert, Willet E. White.

Additional Reading

The reader may wish to consult the *National Geographic Index* for related articles and books. The following may also prove useful: Elna S. Bakker, *An Island Called California: An Ecological Introduction to its Natural Communities;* C. S. Beals, editor, *Science, History and Hudson Bay, Volumes* 1 and 2; Frans Blom and Gertrude Duby, *La Selva Lacandona;* Kenneth Brower, *Earth and the Great Weather: The Brooks Range;* George Calef, *Caribou and the Barren-Lands;* Catherine Caufield, *In the Rain Forest;* Stan Cohen and Don Miller, *The Big Burn: The Northwest's Forest Fire of 1910;* John W. Hakola, *A Legacy of Time;* Dewitt Jones and Linda S. Cordell, *Anasazi World;* Barry Lopez, *Arctic Dreams;* James A. MacMahon, *The Audubon Society Nature Guides: Deserts;* Frank McNitt, *Richard Wetherill: Anasazi;* Roderick Nash, *Wilderness and the American Mind;* Parks Canada, *Indian and Northern Affairs, Wild Rivers: James Bay and Hudson Bay;* Stephen J. Pyne, *Fire in America: A Cultural History of Wildland and Rural Fire;* Henry D. Thoreau, *The Maine Woods;* B. Traven, *March to the Monteria;* Arthur C. Twomey, *Needle to the North.*

Library of Congress CIP Data

America's hidden wilderness.
  Bibliography: p.
  Includes index.
  1. Wilderness areas—North America. I. National Geographic Society (U.S.). Special Publications Division.
QH76.A45 1988   917   88-9977
ISBN 0-87044-666-5 (regular edition)
ISBN 0-87044-671-1 (library edition)

Composition for *America's Hidden Wilderness* by the Typographic section of National Geographic Production Services, Pre-Press Division. Printed and bound by Holladay-Tyler Printing Corp., Rockville, Md. Film preparation by Catharine Cooke Studio, Inc., New York, N.Y. Color separations by Lanman Progressive Company, Washington, D.C.; Lincoln Graphics, Inc. Cherry Hill, N.J.; and NEC, Inc. Nashville, Tenn. Case cover and dust jacket printed by Federated Lithographers-Printers, Inc., Providence, R.I.

Index

Boldface indicates illustrations.